Shayne
&
Stacey.

Enjoy the life you
have every single day because
you never Know what tomorrow
brings. It can all change in a
Split Second.

Sandra (Hocking) McAvoy

Split Second

Split-Second Life Change

Sandra Hocking

iUniverse, Inc.
Bloomington

Split Second
Split-Second Life Change
Shattered Future: September 11, 2004

iUniverse books may be ordered through booksellers or by contacting:

iUniverse
1663 Liberty Drive
Bloomington, IN 47403
www.iuniverse.com
1-800-Authors (1-800-288-4677)

ISBN: 978-1-4759-6194-2 (sc)
ISBN: 978-1-4759-6195-9 (hc)
ISBN: 978-1-4759-6196-6 (e)

Library of Congress Control Number: 2012921345

Printed in the United States of America

iUniverse rev. date: 11/27/2012

I would like to dedicate this book to my remarkable husband Raymond Hocking. He has taught me more in these last eight years than I have learned in the fifty-nine years prior. With his wisdom, patience and understanding of human nature, he has been able to endure this hardship with the knowledge that he will rely on others for the rest of his life. He is generally optimistic and looks forward to more tomorrows. He accepts life for what it is and has told me more times than I can count.…..**don't try to change something you can't.**

I want to thank my wonderful daughter, Gina Marie, for putting me in touch with a lady who read my rough draft and offered her expert advice on improving the structure of my manuscript. Thank you, Theresa, for your expertise.

I owe a debt of gratitude to my good friend Laurel Giesing, who was always available to assist. She was my sounding board as well as my computer genius. Without her, I would never have had an accepted manuscript.

Rebekka Potter was my contact at iUniverse and I want to thank her for all her help and guidance every step of the way. Also, the editing and publishing staff deserves a thank you. Everyone I spoke with was very pleasant and encouraged me throughout the process.

Prologue

Family is where your story begins.

I can't remember a time when I wasn't in love. Bill, my first true love, and I graduated from high school in 1962 and started dating shortly after. Two years later we were married and vowed to spend the rest of our lives together. As long as I can remember, the only thing I ever wanted to be was a mother. When all attempts to become parents failed, we gave up all hope of ever having a child. Finally, after ten and a half years of marriage, we had the privilege of welcoming our precious daughter, Gina Marie, into our lives. I knew then that all those years had been worth the wait, especially when this adorable little girl put her arms around my neck and hugged me. My life was perfect. But then I found out that all good things come to an end. After twenty-two years of marriage, Bill and I divorced. My heart was broken, and I was convinced that I would never find love again … until Raymond Hocking came into my life.

CHAPTER 1

||||||||||||||||||||||||||||||||||||||||||||||||||||||||||||||||||||||||||||||||||||||||||||||||||

The Beginning

When you realize you want to spend the rest
of your life with somebody, you want
the rest of your life to start as soon as possible.
Billy Crystal

We met on a hot August day in 1986 in a little neighborhood sports bar where I had been bartending for a couple of years. As I opened the door at 11:30 a.m., a few construction linemen who were working in the area were ready for their lunch break. I was immediately attracted to the handsome curly-haired, bearded gentleman who ordered a hamburger with mayonnaise. I promptly told him that we do not serve mayo on burgers in this bar. Here they are eaten with ketchup! When he realized I was joking, we both laughed, and that was the beginning of our friendly conversations.

Since he was working close by, He started coming in regularly, and I looked forward to seeing him. He was easy to talk to and not too bad to look at either, especially with those ocean-blue eyes and coal-black beard. We talked about our families, and I learned that he'd grown up in Denville, New Jersey, was the oldest of two sons, and sadly, both of his parents were deceased. Two years after he and his wife married, they relocated to California, bought a house in San Clemente, and he found a job at the power company. They never had children, so when his twenty-year marriage ended, he left his job and joined the IBEW (International Brotherhood of Electrical Workers), which brought him to Connecticut. Since he had traveled all over the United States and had never heard of this town, he decided to accept the work in our growing community.

I told him I had grown up with a strict Italian father and three younger siblings. My brothers Richard and Michael were three and ten years younger, respectively, and my sister Debra arrived when I was approaching thirteen. I was married at the age of nineteen, my daughter was born when I was thirty, and I was forty-two when I became a single mom.

One evening we went out for coffee and realized how much we enjoyed each other's company. After dating a short time, we knew we wanted this relationship to last. I introduced him to my daughter, and we began including her in many of the things we did. Introducing him to my parents was another matter, especially my father, who thought Ray was taking advantage of me and called him a "drifter." My brother Dick, who became very fond of Ray, told my father that Ray was serious and eventually wanted to marry me. After that, Ray was like one of the family.

We had a short courtship and got married on August 2, 1987, the one-year anniversary of the day we met, with my daughter as my maid of honor. Even though she was only twelve, I wanted to include her in this important event. She understood that just because there was a new man in my life, she was still very special. I also talked with Ray, letting him know that Gina and I were a package deal, and he promised a great future for the three of us. When Gina and I went shopping for my wedding dress and her maid of honor dress, we had a great afternoon together. It was difficult choosing between so many gorgeous dresses, but in the end we must have made the right decision, because we were both told we looked beautiful. My niece Dina wanted to be in the wedding, so she was the ring bearer. We purchased a dress exactly like Gina's for her, and the two looked like little angels.

We were married at my parents' home with only immediate family and a few close friends in attendance, and then we left for our honeymoon. After flying into Reno, Nevada, we rented a car and drove along the coast from Reno to Los Angeles where we stayed for a few days at my cousin David's home and had an absolutely wonderful time. Next, Ray took me to meet the men he had worked with at the power company. We joined them in a bar, which I quickly learned was where linemen tended to hang out. He introduced me to sushi in Malibu and took me to his favorite Mexican restaurant in San Clemente. We shopped in San Juan Capistrano and saw the cable cars in San Francisco. We drove through the quaint town of Carmel, where Clint Eastwood was mayor. I gambled, playing poker in a casino in Reno—and won! We had a fabulous ten days, but I was eager to get home to my daughter and start my new life.

Once back home, we settled in quite comfortably and I learned what a wonderful cook Ray was. He enjoyed cooking foods for me, many of which I had never even heard of. I remember when he asked me if I had a wok. I had no idea what he was referring to, but it became one of our most used kitchen utensils. I also liked to cook, so most of our time together was spent in the kitchen. On Gina's thirteenth birthday, she had several friends over, and Ray made cheese fondue for a bread dip and chocolate fondue to dip strawberries. None of them had had fondue before, so it was a big hit! Surprisingly, Gina liked many of the new foods Ray cooked, which frequently contained garlic, onions, and everything hot and spicy.

The first time he made spaghetti sauce, I was amazed at the amount of onions and garlic he used—enough to fill half the pot. It certainly did the trick because the sauce was out of this world. One evening when he was cooking, my parents stopped by and our house reeked of garlic. My father said, "That's the way a house should smell!" Ray also made martinis better than anyone I know, and his margaritas were to die for. Boy, do I miss those drinks.

Many evenings when he served dinner, he lit candles on the table or added a vase of beautiful flowers, and there was always a glass of great-tasting wine.

Gina moved out when she was twenty, and a few weeks later I started feeling depressed and out of sorts. After I got over my empty-nest syndrome though, Ray and I became accustomed to life without Gina. A few years later, she decided to move to her boyfriend's home state of Minnesota. I cried for days. I was planning on seeing her off but was so sad about her leaving that I could not go to say good-bye. Ray was so supportive and tried to make it a little easier for me by cooking a wonderful dinner the day she left. He even went out that night and brought back my favorite treat—pistachio ice cream. For the next couple of years, every time Gina had to leave after being home for a visit, I cried. The first year she was gone, we drove out to Minneapolis to spend part of the Christmas holiday with her. When it was time for me to leave, I couldn't stop the tears. As the years went on, I learned to live without her being near, and the good-byes got a little easier.

Ray did not like to fly, so we did all our traveling by car. Our first cross-country trip was in 1989. Ray enjoyed showing me the country he loved, and that trip was one of the greatest experiences of my life and the one I treasure the most. It was an amazing drive, being alone with the person you love, with no interruptions, just relaxing and enjoying the sights. What a luxury!

We drove to California a few times, to my aunt's in Arizona, to my daughter's in Minneapolis, to a resort in the Rockies in Colorado, to Ray's relatives in Wyoming, where we also visited Yellowstone National Park. Closer to home, we traveled to New Jersey to visit more of Ray's relatives. We've often said that we're so glad we traveled to those wonderful places instead of waiting until after retirement, like so many people do. Our last road trip was in May 2004, when we went to Arizona to celebrate my Aunt Rainey's eightieth birthday. Of course, at the time we had no idea it would be our last.

Several years after we were married, I wrote this article about what I was thankful for at Thanksgiving. It appeared in our local newspaper.

It Just Doesn't Get Better Than This

I am especially thankful this year because I feel that I have accomplished the one thing that I never thought was possible for me—a job that I love with a great salary. Some of the people I work with have become very special to me, and I know will be for the rest of my life. During my 56 years, there have been a few friends that have endured the ups and downs of my life's journey, which at times were turbulent. Knowing that these special friends were there when I needed them gives me a very warm feeling inside.

As everyone knows, however, happiness begins at home. I feel very lucky that my elderly parents are healthy and happy and were able to provide the foundation for me to become the well-adjusted person that I feel I am. They also gave me two wonderful brothers and a sister whom I adore. Together we have contributed many wonderful additions to this already "perfect" family. My contribution is a beautiful daughter who has grown into a woman who makes me burst with pride at her accomplishments. Last but not least, I have the love of a wonderful man, my husband, who tells me every day, how very much he loves me

This is a special year to be thankful because I feel that it can't get better than this.

In 2003, we decided it was time to move out of the rented condo we lived in and buy our own place. We looked at several properties and decided to purchase a condo. Neither of us liked yard work, and in hindsight a condo was the perfect choice. Ray went to an open house at a new development one Sunday while I was working, liked what he saw, and made an appointment for me to see it. The kitchen won me over! Since it's our favorite room and most of our time is spent there, it wasn't too difficult to imagine us cooking our favorite meals in that great big kitchen. How ironic that Ray would fall in the room he loved best.

We moved in on December 19, 2003, and Gina flew in from Minnesota on December 23. We had our traditional family gathering on Christmas Eve. Everyone loved our new place, even though we still had a lot of boxes to unpack. Of course there was a room for Gina, with a beautiful new queen-size bed and her own bathroom.

Since my workday ended at 8:30 p.m., the only time Ray and I had a meal together was on my days off. Those two days were very special to us, and we looked forward to them each week. Our routine was for him to fix me one of his famous margaritas, which I would enjoy while sitting at the computer and reading e-mails while he cooked our dinner. Once in a while he would create some exotic hors d'oeuvre to accompany the margarita.

Those days only lasted nine months. Our condo was brand new and we were full of ideas as to how we were going to finish decorating each room. Those rooms are still waiting.

CHAPTER 2

The Accident

... stepping from the known to the unknown.
George Shinn

It was a routine Saturday. Ray worked until about two in the afternoon and then went to his favorite gathering place, a quaint lounge he had discovered months earlier.

After some friendly conversation and his favorite cocktail, he went home and made a stir-fry for dinner. When he finished eating, he cleaned up the kitchen and then called me at Mohegan Sun Casino, where I'd been working for the past six years, to say he was going to relax on the couch and read his book until I got home. That's where I found him when I walked through the door at 9:00 p.m. We talked for a while, and then I picked up my soap opera magazine and began reading too. Approximately a half hour later, he went into the kitchen to get two spoons and a half gallon of ice cream, which was one of our favorite treats. As usual, we consumed more than we should have, remarking about the calorie intake while trying to convince ourselves that it also contained ingredients that were good for us. Ray put the remainder back in the freezer and said he was tired and was going up to bed. I asked him to stay with me for just a while longer, so he sat back down, pretended to read his book, and fell asleep.

Approximately an hour later I finished my magazine and decided to call it a day. Ray was sleeping peacefully, so I left him there and went upstairs, thinking of that nice big king-size bed I would have all to myself. Little did I know that I would never sleep with him again in that bed, or any other bed. Since that night I've told people never to wish for something because it may just come true!

I was brushing my teeth when I was startled by what sounded like a *thud*. I listened for a few seconds, but hearing nothing more, I continued brushing. When I finished, I thought I should investigate, so I walked down the stairs. Ray was not on the couch where I had left him, so I softly called his name.

"Sandra, I'm in here," he answered.

I walked into the kitchen, but couldn't see him because of the counter divider we recently had installed. "Where are you?" I asked. When he answered, "Over here," I looked around the corner by the kitchen sink. He was lying on his back on the floor.

"What the hell are you doing down there?" I asked.

He said he'd woken up and gone into the kitchen to get some orange juice. As he lifted the container and tipped his head back to take a sip, he fell backward and landed flat on his back. He asked me to help him up. I grabbed his hand, but he immediately said, "Forget it. Call 911 and tell them I just fell and broke my neck and I'm paralyzed."

Stunned, I asked, "How do you know you broke your neck?"

"Because I heard it snap!"

The paramedics arrived immediately. A neighbor, who happened to be a nurse, came running as soon as she saw the ambulance approaching our condo. She assisted as they put a neck brace on him and pricked his body with a needle, trying to determine a loss of sensation. At that point, he had no feeling below the "nipple" line, and he muttered, "I'm going to be just like Superman." Another neighbor hurried over. She stayed with me until Ray was in the ambulance and on the way to the hospital. We followed in her car, and I called my parents, my brother Dick, and my sister Debby, explaining that Ray had fallen and I was with my neighbor following the ambulance and would they come as soon as they could. My brother Mike was on vacation and found out the following day. Coincidentally, my daughter was visiting us from Minneapolis, en route to a friend's wedding in Maine. At the time of the accident she was at another friend's party and planned to spend the night. Naturally, my call upset her. She wanted to come to the hospital to be with me, but I assured her I was not alone. I didn't want her driving at that hour; it was now approaching midnight.

After arriving at the hospital, we waited for about an hour until we were allowed in to see Ray. The image of him will be with me forever! He had a contraption on his head that was screwed into his skull, and those beautiful blue eyes of his followed me around the room as the doctor showed me the X-rays and told me in a tone I will never forget: "He's paralyzed." It was a good thing my brother was there, because all the life went out of me, and he caught me as I fell into a chair.

"His paralysis is at C4/C5," the doctor said, which meant nothing to me at that time.

The nurse asked me what that pink stuff was that they had pumped out of his stomach. I realized it was the cherry vanilla ice cream we had devoured about two hours earlier!

The same nurse took me aside and told me that from now on our lives would never be the same. I would have a rough road ahead of me. She said, after Ray realizes the extent of his injury, he isn't going to want to live. He's going to feel sorry for himself and wonder, Why me? She was right about our lives never being the same. However, she was not right about Ray feeling sorry for himself. For reasons unknown, he has never been depressed about his situation.

He's a remarkable man, and I'm so proud of him. He's never complained, and believe me, with what he endures daily, he has every right! I've had to turn away many times so he wouldn't see the tears in my eyes. I keep thinking to myself, If there's a God up there, why would a wonderful man like Ray have to go through such an ordeal? The simplest things that people take for granted, like brushing their teeth or picking up a fork to eat, were taken from him forever. That night at the hospital I tried to put out of my mind what it would be like to never have him put his arms around me again. A little hug at the end of the day was my safest and most comfortable place, and that would never, ever be again.

My brother brought me home from the hospital about four in the morning. I couldn't bring myself to climb the stairs to our bedroom. The way I felt, I didn't think I could ever go in that room and look at that bed, knowing we would never sleep in it together again. I sat on the couch and called Mohegan Sun Casino, where I was a credit executive, and told them what happened. Since the casino is open twenty-four hours, there's always someone there. I was advised to call the human resources department on Monday and get the necessary paperwork for a medical leave of absence.

I sat on the couch in a daze until my niece, Dina, arrived around six in the morning, still clad in her pajamas. She helped me make the necessary phone calls to Ray's employer, his relatives, and his friends while my sister called my relatives. It was difficult breaking the news because, at that time, I really didn't know what the complete prognosis was.

I also contacted his friends and coworkers in San Diego, and to this day, many have followed his progress via phone calls, e-mails, and visits.

The next day Gina went with me to see him in the Critical Care Unit (CCU), also known as the trauma ward, where he spent the next two weeks going in and out of consciousness. I escorted her because I wanted to make sure she wouldn't be frightened when she saw the apparatus surrounding his head. He was able to talk to us and didn't seem to be in any pain. She stayed for quite a while, until I was told that someone else was in the waiting room wanting to see him. Since only two visitors were allowed at a time, I walked her out.

She was at the hospital daily, and I thought she was handling it well until I caught her in tears one day when we went out for some much needed fresh air. I knew her friend who was getting married was counting on her, and that she needed a break from the stress of seeing Ray and worrying about me, so I was glad when it was time for her to leave for the wedding.

One day my brother and I were in the room when a doctor came in and started poking different parts of Ray's body. We saw his foot move after one of these pokes and we were ecstatic, but the doctor assured us that it was an involuntary movement and that we could expect to see them throughout his lifetime.

Our good friends, Carol and Stan, sat with me in the waiting room on Monday, September 13, during the operation to repair the neck. After three long hours the doctor finally called to say that Ray had made it through the surgery and was "resting comfortably." He said he had inserted a breathing tube, and that Ray would need to wear a collar for two months. He asked if I thought he could tolerate that. My reply was, "Absolutely not!" Ray proved me wrong because he wore that collar and never complained once.

On Tuesday, the day after the operation, he was very restless until I realized he was trying to say something. It took a while before I understood that he wanted a pencil and paper since he couldn't speak because of the breathing tube in his mouth. All I told him was that his hands didn't work right now.

I received this e-mail from my niece Jenny, my brother Mike's daughter, on Wednesday, September 15:

I am sincerely sorry about Ray. Michael called me Sunday morning to tell me the news and my mom updated me after she and my father went to the hospital. I feel bad being far away. We get so wrapped up in our own lives that we never think bad things will happen to the ones we love. You sound very strong in your message, and I don't know if I could be that strong. I send my love and best wishes and hope Ray will handle it all well when he realizes what is going on. I will pray for you and Ray and Gina and everyone who has supported you since this happened. Stay strong and positive. Miracles do happen if we trust in God.

The jeans that Ray had worn on his last day of work were lying on the chair in the bedroom needing to be laundered. I threw them in the machine with other clothes and forgot about them. What a surprise when the cycle was over and I took the clothes out of the washer. I discovered money, lots of money, that obviously had been in his pockets. I wasn't in the habit of going through his pockets because he always emptied them himself. I found dollar bills in every denomination from one to one hundred. When I took the clothes out of the dryer, I found more money—$850 in all! Ray never carried more than a couple of dollars in his pockets, so where the hell had all this money come from? Many weeks later I found out that it was money from his overtime checks, which was what he saved for our vacations. He hadn't made it to the bank yet to put the money in our vacation fund. However, that money carried me through the next three months of not working. He had about twelve weeks of accumulated sick leave too, so I received his paycheck in the mail every week until I went back to work.

The second operation was performed on Friday, September 17. The breathing tube was replaced with a respirator, a feeding tube was implanted in his stomach, which enabled him to consume a protein liquid, and a filter was inserted to prevent blood clots. Eighteen bags of different medicines hung around him, some empty, some ready to be intravenously emptied into his body.

He developed pneumonia while in intensive care and had to have his lungs drained periodically. Late one night, when my brother and I were there, he started choking, and it looked like he was actually foaming at the mouth. I summoned the nurse, and she made us leave. I didn't think I was ever going to see him alive again!

By Saturday, September 18, a week after the accident, I couldn't believe the overwhelming support from family and friends. I received cards from well-wishers by the handfuls every day, some from people I didn't even know but who had heard about the accident through others. There were also phone messages every evening when I returned home. In fact, one night there were twenty-eight messages! Two of his good friends from California, as well as his brother, called when

I happened to be at home and I was glad I had the opportunity to speak with them.

During his two weeks in CCU, his visitors were allowed to stay for only ten minutes. Outside of the family, his boss and his coworkers were his first visitors. These men visited often, and Ray loved being updated about the happenings in the lineman's world, even though he doesn't remember anything of the time he was in CCU. However, these men were frequent visitors and offered to help me in any way possible.

His cousin Lois, whom he was close with, was naturally concerned and wanted to see him and help and comfort me. She lived in Pennsylvania and came on Sunday, September 19, and stayed with me for a week. Most days we sat together in his hospital room while trying to figure out a way to communicate with him. She drew a chart with the letters of the alphabet and would point to them whenever he wanted to tell us something. Her presence also gave me the opportunity to accomplish things that I had been putting off, because I hadn't wanted to leave him for too long. I needed guidance in legal matters, most importantly, as my father suggested, to become Ray's power of attorney, since he was now unable to write. I also had to deliver the completed papers to my employer for a medical leave of absence. I was told that I had to take my accrued vacation first, which consisted of one week, and was then was allowed a twelve-week medical leave, with a return-to-work date of December 18, 2004.

When it was finally time for Gina to go back to Minneapolis, I knew leaving me would be one of the hardest things she'd ever had to do in her young life. Her father was taking her to the airport, and I told him to reassure her of the support I had so her mind would be somewhat at ease. I hated to see her go, but I'll always remember something she had said to me a few days earlier. We were standing in my kitchen and she said, "Mom, I know you're going to make it through this because you're a nurturer. You like caring for people. And now you have Sam. She's very good for you and she loves you very much."

She was referring to Samanthia Mauro, my good young friend from work who'd been especially helpful to me since the beginning of this traumatic situation and, ironically, would soon become an addition to my family.

My nephew Richard, my brother Dick's son, came from California a week after the accident. It seemed that Ray was asleep every time Richard visited him. Finally, just before Richard had to return to California, Ray opened his eyes. Richard rubbed his head, and as they looked into each other's eyes, Richard said, "Thanks for waking up. I love you, Ray. You're one of my favorite people. That's why I came across the country to see you. We're all behind you and will pray for you and help you any way we can." It was a very touching scene and will be etched in my memory forever.

After Richard returned to California, I sent him an e-mail telling him how much I appreciated him traveling all that way to see Ray, and how amazing he was on that last night when Ray finally woke up. This is his reply to my e-mail:

You don't have to thank me for coming ... but you're welcome anyways ... I had to come ... the second this whole tragedy that had happened to Ray hit me ... and it took about 36 hours before it truly sank in ... in my head I was already on my way, it was just a matter of logistics to get back there. And as you know ... I haven't been able to shake that time I was able to see and talk with Ray either ... it's pretty emblazoned in my head ... I'm sure it will always be. I've been thinking about Ray a lot ... I'm not talking a lot about it ... but mostly I can't seem to shake Ray from my thoughts ... it's just so unfair what has happened to him. It just doesn't make any sense to me. And when I think about Ray ... I immediately think about Tiffany and Gracey and Jack ... and if something similar ever happened to them someday ... just any old normal day ... and how a 3 year old could even begin to process something like that happening. Jeez ... it's just so sad, Sandy. It's just so sad ... very sad. That's the best way I can begin to explain it ... it's simply sad. It makes me sad to think about. Please tell Ray I said hello and that we're pulling for him out here in his beloved Southern California … and let him know that I'll be back …I told him I'd be back to see him and I will … it probably won't be until sometime after the holidays … but I promised him I'd bring some SoCal back to him this winter to warm him up a bit.

Throughout the two weeks in CCU, many of my friends, relatives, and coworkers came daily to sit with me in the waiting room during the hour in the morning and again in the afternoon when I was not allowed in because they were tending to Ray's needs. Some brought food so I wouldn't forget to eat, and many waited to take their turn to visit him for the allotted ten minutes. Some were there just to lend their support because they were not ready to see him yet. I understood and appreciated the fact that they were there with me at that time when I really didn't want to be alone. My Aunt Rainey and Uncle Joe from Arizona were visiting at the time of Ray's accident, and they made it to the hospital during the first week in CCU.

During this time, family members were concerned about me. They thought I should call my doctor and explain the situation, which I finally did. He prescribed a medication that would help me relax. One day it relaxed me so much, I fell asleep in the waiting room! From then on, I made sure the only time I took a pill was at night.

Before she left, Gina and I met with a case worker at the hospital, one of the people specially trained to speak with family members of critically injured patients. I was considering moving Ray to a specialty hospital, as suggested by his niece, who was a trauma nurse in Pennsylvania. We were advised not to move him because of the severity of his condition.

My brother wanted more information about the breathing apparatus, so the doctor arranged a meeting that my brother, Lois, and I attended on Monday, September 20. The doctor told us he didn't know if the respirator would be permanent. The only definite thing was that Ray was paralyzed and that was not going to change because he'd had a complete break of the spinal cord, which meant it was severed and could not be repaired. Even though we'd known he would always be paralyzed, it was still heartbreaking to hear that again, because we still didn't know what we were facing.

For the two weeks in CCU, his lungs continued to fill with fluid and had to be suctioned often. During those times he was conveniently incoherent, unaware of what was happening. The doctor showed Lois and me a computer X-ray of his lungs, while explaining the seriousness of pneumonia and its constant threat in the future.

Ray continued to sleep most of the time. One day I happened to look over at him and saw a frown on his face, and then a tear appeared in his right eye. I glanced at the monitor to make sure he wasn't getting excited. His blood pressure, heart rate, and oxygen level were all normal, so I assumed there was no cause for alarm.

On Saturday, September 25, two weeks after his accident and while Ray was still in CCU, after he had been "asleep" for a few days, he seemed very anxious. I thought it was because he was trying to understand what was happening. I couldn't imagine what was going on inside his head. I just wanted him to know I was there. I went to the hospital gift shop and bought a balloon, and I made sure it was placed where he could see it at all times.

Another day he opened his eyes and looked directly at me. I told him, "You look much better today. Don't try to talk with that contraption in your mouth. Go back to sleep and dream about me. Try to remember what your dream is about because I'm going to write a book about this someday."

His beautiful blue eyes told me he understood, and then he closed them again and went back to dreaming.

I kept a close watch on the monitor and became familiar with its beeps. When he became agitated, the monitor would make a scary sound, and I knew it meant the nurse had to be summoned so she could make an adjustment. The monitor recorded his heartbeat, blood pressure, pulse, and respirations, and I made daily comparisons and became familiar with the changes. Whenever his breathing became irregular, a nurse gave him one medication to calm him. That would increase his blood pressure, so he needed another medication to control that. It was a vicious circle.

I let the staff in CCU know that I was adamant about anyone shaving his beard. However, one day when I arrived, a care attendant asked me how I liked his new look. When I realized she had shaved some of his beard, I almost wrapped my fingers around her neck!

"What did you do that for?" I yelled.

She said one side of his face had to be shaved because of the breathing apparatus, so she thought she should even out the look and shave the other side. I didn't know how I was going to tell him. I loved the beard and had never seen him without it. When we talked about it weeks later, his response was that it really didn't matter anymore as there were more important issues to be concerned about.

After two weeks in CCU, Ray was transferred to a private room for what they called continuing care. That's when I started staying overnight with him. One night he begged me not to leave, and the nurse said it would be all right if I stayed. Of course, that was the beginning of my sleepless nights, and shortly after that I learned to exist on practically no sleep at all. It was a reminder of the days when my daughter was little and I would be up all night with her.

During this time, my coworker and good friend Samanthia had become a very important person in my life, like another daughter.. She was at my house constantly, cooking for me, washing clothes, making my bed, and doing whatever else she could think of to make my life a little easier. I was receiving e-mails daily and received a special one from her on September 30:

> I have been thinking of Ray all day. I think the swelling is starting to come down and perhaps he'll have some feeling, wouldn't that be excellent? Please don't think for one second that I didn't want to stay with you tonight. I thought maybe you wanted some time to yourself. Don't worry, I'll be back tomorrow. I don't want you to have too much time by yourself. I felt so bad yesterday when you were crying. It is

*Sandra

so emotionally draining. Even if you get the best sleep in the world you are thinking continuously all day and that can be even more tiring than not getting any sleep. One day at a time, Sandra, that's all I can say. I'm sure you are going to have many more up and down days but no matter what, I will be there. Please don't hesitate to ask me for anything. I can't do stuff if you don't ask. We want to help so any little thing even if you think it is stupid, please ask. Cleaning, cooking, or whatever you want, I will do it. Please let me help. You have done more for me than anyone has, and I want to return that favor. I'm not sure what I did to have God bless me with a friend like you but I'm glad he did. You are amazing. I read your card and was thinking that I should be thanking you for all you have done for me but then I came to realize that maybe we need each other to get through things in life and that's fine with me. I couldn't ask for a better friend. Ray is so lucky to have someone like you by his side and even though sometimes the future looks bleak there is no way that it can with you in the picture. You are unbelievable, and I don't think Ray could get through this if it was with someone else. It's okay that you can't be strong all the time, I don't think he expects you to. You have every right to be mad and angry and cry and everything else that goes on with this emotional roller coaster but when you are weak Ray will be strong and you guys will carry each other further then you ever thought you could. I guess both of you are what marriage is really about and you and Ray have taught me that there is so much more to life then materialistic things. I think you and Ray have taught a lot of people things in the past two weeks. Love is powerful and the love that you both have for each other is stronger than any physical ailment on this earth. I think my mom would be proud that I have friends like you and Ray :-) I love you! I will talk to you soon! Let me know if you need anything—Okay?

During this time I was e-mailing my coworkers each week with updates, and I received this touching message from Janis, also on September 30:

Hi Sandra ... Just read the e-mail that you wrote the other day. I am so glad to hear Ray is making progress, no matter how small, on his road to recovery. All these little things will start adding up. I hope you don't stop e-mailing us every week because I look forward to hearing from you directly on how things are going. I had to print the first letter you wrote and show it to Michael ... I was just so moved by the love and determination that came through what you wrote. Anyways, maybe you won't have guests next Tuesday and I can make some lunch and bring it by?!?!?! As always, my thoughts are with you. :-)

One day my niece came to see Ray and brought her baby with her. A little while after she arrived, the baby started crying, so I took her for a walk to the family waiting room. While I was there, I had a friendly conversation with a gentleman in a wheelchair. At the time, I did not know what a good friend and a great help he would become to both Ray and me.

A representative from a rehabilitation facility in a neighboring town visited. He informed us that Ray was a good candidate for them and they would be waiting to welcome him upon his release from this hospital.

CHAPTER 3

Rehabilitation

Change of any sort requires courage.
Mary Anne Radmacher

After spending twenty-five days in the hospital, Ray was transferred to the rehabilitation facility. I rode in the ambulance with him while my brother drove my car and my sister followed in hers. We arrived in the early afternoon on Wednesday, October 6, 2004, at the place that would be his home for the next thirty-five days. It was a very emotional day for me, the first of many to come. Ray was taken into a room for an evaluation, and a team of doctors and nurses came in and introduced themselves. During the evaluation they discovered a stage two bedsore on his lower back. They told us they would make every effort to heal it so that it didn't develop into a wound.

He was admitted to the pulmonary unit and was weaned off the ventilator in a short time. On Wednesday, October 13, the ventilator hose was removed and a valve was inserted in the hole in his throat. This enabled him to speak for the first time in a month. What a relief that was, because every time he had needed my attention before, he made a crazy sound with his lips. Once in a while he'll make that sound now, because he knows how much I grew to hate it and we joke about it. Now that he could speak, we had our first conversation about his paralysis and how it had changed our life. Since Ray was prone to congestion, it was difficult for him to cough and relieve his lungs of fluid. A nurse could remove the valve and insert a suction tube that would reach down into his lungs.

We were still puzzled about the fact that he was a quadriplegic, since we had thought a severed spine could somehow be fixed. I had not read about stem cell research and didn't know the President's position on the subject. However, I began to research Ray's condition on the Internet and became intrigued by the Christopher Reeve Foundation, especially Dana Reeve's position as her husband's caregiver. I called and was told that the foundation couldn't do anymore for my husband than this facility.

Ray's next step was the spinal cord unit for intense therapy on his arms and legs. The patient was there for rehabilitation, but they also taught the family members how to care for their loved ones. The physical therapist taught me how to perform the range of motion exercises on his arms and legs, which had to be done every day, as well as on his fingers, hands, toes, and feet. I also had to learn the correct way to turn him, which is very important for a paralyzed person since it takes only two hours for a bedsore to form. He had a special air mattress with a motor that forced the air throughout the bed to ease the pressure points, which are shoulders, elbows, knees, hips, heels, and coccyx—which was where Ray's bedsore was.

We learned of a condition that commonly affects individuals with spinal cord injuries, at or above T6, called autonomic dysreflexia, which is a medical emergency that requires immediate attention. It occurs when a sensation below the level of the spinal cord lesion, that would normally be painful, causes excessive reflex activity in the autonomic nervous system. The nervous system maintains functions in metabolism, cardiovascular activity, temperature regulation, and digestion. If the cause of the dysreflexia is not found and treated, the patient's blood pressure can rise to dangerously high levels, possibly resulting in brain hemorrhage, fits, and heart palpitations. Autonomic dysreflexia presents with several symptoms: sudden rise in blood pressure, severe pounding headache, bradycardia (very slow pulse), flushing or blotching of the skin on the head and neck, sweating, goose bumps, nasal stuffiness, blurred vision, chills without fever, shortness of breath, and anxiety. The common causes are a distended bladder, blocked catheter, urinary tract infection, constipation, pressure sores, burns, ingrown toenails, tight clothing, fractures, kidney stones, labor, menstrual pain, and distended stomach. Everyone caring for Ray had to be able to recognize these signs and understand that every instance was an emergency.

Since he had no control over his body, he was put on a bowel program. Every night at approximately 6:30, he was given a suppository. We hoped for a movement in two hours, otherwise the nurse would push on his stomach and, with a gloved hand, probe the sphincter muscle and wait to see if he eliminated. If not, every effort was made to help the situation manually. If nothing was produced, the nurse would try again in another hour or so. We grew to hate this part of the evening because, not only was it embarrassing, many times it interfered with our dinner or interrupted phone calls that we wanted or needed to make. However, it was a program we knew would eventually benefit him.

I stayed every night. When I had to attend to something at home, I would leave in the morning after breakfast and try to be back in time to feed him dinner. One day when I returned, he had a paper sign lying across the bed that one of the nurses had made that said "I missed you."

On October 14, which was his ninth day in rehab, his care coordinator gave us a tentative release date of November 23. She said he would have to go to a skilled nursing facility before going home. I asked if "skilled nursing facility" was a glorified name for a convalescent home. It seems that was what they were known as now! This was a shock, because we had thought he would be going home from the rehab center. A nursing home! Those were for old people, not someone as young as Ray.

Although the medical team made every effort to heal the bedsore, their attempts were futile. It became a stage four bedsore and was now a wound. We were told a "wound vac" was needed to try to heal this fist-sized hole on his coccyx. One day while they were changing his bandages, I decided to be brave and peek at it. After that, I never looked again. It was a scary sight! A plastic surgeon came in to offer his opinion. After examining Ray, the surgeon said he needed to have a flap surgery, which is a technique in plastic and reconstructive surgery in which any type of tissue is lifted from a donor site to a recipient site with an intact blood supply. This operation was scheduled for November 11, 2004.

After thirty-five days at the rehabilitation facility, we left at 10:00 the night of November 10. Ray was immediately admitted to a hospital for his surgery, scheduled for the next day. We were supposed to have left rehab at 9:00, but there had been a mix-up at the hospital. Ray needed a special bed, and there was only one available *after* another patient had been discharged. We were also told that he would have to go to a nursing care facility (convalescent home) for the six-week recuperation period. However, the surgeon said the facility we had chosen was out of the question because it was too far for him to check on Ray. The case worker arranged with our insurance company for Ray to stay at the hospital for the entire recuperation time.

My sister Debby sat with me during the four hours he spent in the operating room and five and a half hours in the recovery room. His surgery required forty-six stitches and twenty-seven staples. After his first three hours in the recovery room, we were allowed in. His body temperature was low, only ninety-five degrees. They had heating pads on him, and he was finally allowed to go to his room about six o'clock, with his temperature at ninety-seven degrees. The operation itself was successful, barring no infections in the near future, and we were told the first two weeks were crucial.

I was very happy with the staff there. They were friendly and professional, and I felt at ease immediately. They fell in love with Ray because of his positive attitude and wonderful sense of humor. They enjoyed hanging out in his room because he always made them laugh. His room was next to the nurse's station, with a large glass wall that made it convenient for him to see what was going on. He was in a special bed called a Clinitron bed. It was designed to minimize pressure and distribute weight evenly over its surface. Inside the mattress was a fine sand that was blown around by air when the bed was inflated. Ray did not have to be turned during the six weeks he was on that bed. The only thing needed was a huge wedge behind his back when he sat up to eat, because there were no controls on the bed to raise or lower it. His collar had finally been removed a few days before, which gave him the freedom to turn his head with ease. He knew the names of every medication he was given and the scheduled times when they were administered. He played word games with his surgeon, trying to find a word the surgeon didn't know that he had to look up in the dictionary. The next day the surgeon would come back a little wiser and would try to stump Ray with a word! I would be returning to work before Ray's release, and I was confident he was in good hands.

The plastic surgeon checked on him once a day and always gave a positive assessment. Luckily, there was never an infection. The throat doctor came to see him a few days after the surgery. He put a tube with a light attached to it up his nose and down his throat to check his vocal cords. He said they looked great. Soon he'd be able to be rid of the trachea valve, at which time the hole in his throat would close up and he'd be good as new. At least one part of him would work as before!

During this time, I was trying to settle our personal business and spent a lot of time with my attorney. She said we needed to do a "spend down" so Ray would be able to go on Title 19 and be accepted by Medicaid as soon as possible. She was predicting that he would be hospitalized, requiring long-term care with state assistance. I really had no idea what she was talking about, but knew it would be in my best interest to do as she said. She was the expert in these matters. I did know, however, that if I ran out of money for his care, my home would be taken away from me. I would do everything to make sure that didn't happen! We had 401(k)s, retirement funds, savings accounts, checking accounts, investments, stocks. All but $92,000 had to be liquidated as soon as possible.

Five days after Ray's flap surgery, I was on my way back to the hospital after spending a few hours at home when I stopped for gas.

While I was waiting for an available pump, a tractor trailer truck pulled up alongside of me, a little too close. It attached itself to the driver's side of my Grand Am and pulled me along with him, until his passenger happened to see me out of his rearview mirror. When the trucker finally stopped and we exited our vehicles, we saw the bumper on the driver's side of my car was badly dented. I immediately called my brother, Dick, who had been my saving grace since the beginning of this ordeal, and explained the situation. I told him the truck had a Florida license plate and the driver didn't speak English very well. He told me to call the police, make sure the truck driver didn't leave the scene, and to exchange insurance information, because policemen did not usually respond when called to a "private property" scene. He said he would call a wrecker service and come rescue me. I called the police and told them I needed an officer because of the language barrier. The truck driver got a ticket from the not-so-friendly policeman. I must have disturbed his coffee break.

I had to call Ray. I didn't want to upset him, so I was cautious in what I said. First, I let him know that I was all right, and then I explained the situation. My brother arrived about a half hour later and took me to the hospital. Since I was without a car, Dick made arrangements with a rental company, and I had a Jeep Liberty by morning.

For us there was no Thanksgiving that year. Even though Gina came home, we spent the day with Ray at the hospital, which seemed like just another day.

In order for Ray to be able to leave the hospital, he had to be off bed rest, so on December 15 they started him on a tilt table. It took more than a few people to get him from the bed onto the table. First they put a deflated air mattress under him, inflated it with an electric powered pump, and then pulled him over to the table, where the air mattress was deflated and removed. He was then strapped in with large Velcro straps on his legs and abdomen. The staff had to make an additional strap for his chest with a sheet. Most people have upper body motion and don't need that strap, but since he didn't, the staff had to make its own strap. Once he was strapped in, someone pressed the power button, slowly tilting him upright. They went slowly, allowing him to adjust, until he was at approximately a fifty-degree angle. This was the first step to his rehabilitation. He had been on his back for three months and got dizzy when he sat up, so the tilt table had to be done gradually, so eventually he would be able to sit in a wheelchair.

My medical leave was up while Ray was at the hospital, and I returned to work on December 18. It was quite a change for both of us because we'd been together every day and night for three months. I was looking forward to returning to my job at the casino, but I didn't look forward to being home alone. Five days later, on December 23, 2004, Ray returned to the rehabilitation facility.

Gina came home from Minnesota to spend Christmas with us. We had a small gathering with a few family members in Ray's room for a couple of hours on Christmas Eve, which had always been a special time for us. It was a struggle for me to make it through that evening knowing I would have to leave him alone. Since I had to work the next day, I also wouldn't be able to see him on Christmas Day. He and I were given a few moments of privacy to say our good-byes, and as soon as I left his room, the tears I'd been holding back just poured out. It was one of the worst days of my life, and definitely the worst Christmas Eve I had ever spent. Thankfully, Gina was with me, which made the fifty-minute drive home a little easier. That evening she opened the gifts I had for her while we sat close to the fireplace.

On January 11, 2005, a reporter from our local newspaper came to the rehabilitation facility to interview us because she thought our story would be of public interest. We didn't know at the time how right she was! However, while she was there, Ray's blood pressure suddenly rose dramatically. She could tell how uncomfortable he was and how nervous we both were, and we had to cut her visit short. I apologized and she was very understanding, leaving with the assurance that she would see us very soon. The cause of the rise in Ray's blood pressure was autonomic dysreflexia.

On January 12, 2005, a photographer from the newspaper came and spent about an hour and a half with us. He took several pictures of Ray in the physical therapy area and pictures of both of us as I pushed his stretcher into the elevator and back to his room. He said he would be in touch with us to find out what facility Ray would be transferred to the following week, because he wanted to follow our story.

Unfortunately, the two skilled nursing facilities we had chosen refused to accept Ray, saying they were full. Our choices were limited because of insurance issues and Ray's special needs. We couldn't find a facility that accepted people with injuries such as his, so he had to be placed in a nursing home until—or if—it was determined he'd be able to live at home. There was room for him at a "skilled nursing facility" that was close to our home and my work. A representative came by and spoke with Ray, and said he was a good candidate for their facility and they would be very glad to accommodate us.

I knew once we left the rehabilitation facility, Ray would need a doctor who could take care of him and his special needs. I had been seeing a new doctor that had been recommended to me, and I liked him very much. I called to see if he would also take Ray as a patient. I explained the situation, and he said he would be glad to have Ray. When they met, Ray immediately liked him and put all his faith in the doctor's decisions after that meeting.

CHAPTER 4

||||||||||||||||||||||||||||||||||||||||||||||||||||||||||||||||||||||||||||||||||||||||||||||||||||||

Living at the Nursing Home

Intelligence is the ability to adapt to change.
Stephen Hawking

Ray arrived at the skilled nursing facility in a snowstorm on Wednesday, January 19, 2005. I got there about two hours before him, waiting in the room that would be his home for the unforeseeable future. I was a little anxious because he should have been there before me, but I tried to remain calm. Traffic would be an issue because of the snow. He finally made it and was glad that I was there, in his private room, waiting for him. After he was put to bed, someone brought each of us a turkey sandwich. We were impressed and thought that perhaps this facility wouldn't be so bad after all.

However, the first of many things we discovered was that much of the staff didn't know how to care for a quadriplegic. After all, this was a convalescent home. Most of the residents were old, with many of them suffering from Alzheimer's. I had been taught how to care for Ray so I watched everything the attendants did, making sure they didn't harm his skin in any way, since skin care is very important to a quadriplegic.

A few days after he arrived, I called an acute rehab facility I had discovered on the Internet while researching spinal injuries. The woman I spoke to in the admissions office asked about the level of Ray's injury and if he had the use of his arms. She said I could fax over his information and she would take a look at it, but she didn't think the facility would be able to help him. I did not waste my time sending the information.

After the first few days we realized that if I didn't spend the nights with him, he wasn't going to survive. The first weekend he was there, he was congested and the nurse thought he needed to be suctioned, but this wasn't like the last facility where the equipment was readily available. He had to be transferred to the hospital, which was where he'd spent those first three weeks after his accident. A few hours later, it was back to the nursing home.

Soon after he became a resident, we were told that he was classified as "custodial care," which meant that he was not entitled to physical therapy. Custodial care was maintenance care provided by family members, health aides, or other unlicensed individuals after an acute medical event, in which an individual had reached the maximum level of physical or mental function. Since Ray was not expected to show improvement with his level of injury, the only thing the state claimed he deserved was someone moving his arms and legs daily in range of motion exercises. We were told the nursing assistants would be doing this.

In the beginning they did not take the time to do it, mainly because they didn't have the time. It seemed they were always short-staffed. Plus, they didn't seem to realize how very important this was to his broken body. Because I had been taught, it became a daily task for me. Many days the physical therapy department would let one of their own perform the range of motion exercises. Ray's muscles ached and got very stiff if he didn't have enough range of motion. We soon realized we would have to pay for therapy, so we arranged for him to have a body massage three times a week at a cost of $75 each session—which he thoroughly enjoyed and desperately needed. Anything extra was funded by us.

I get upset about this, because most residents in a "skilled nursing facility" have worked all their lives, fought for their country, have gone without so they could save for retirement, only to end up with nothing but $60 a month to spend on things they either want or need. I hate how the system works, and it's certainly not fair. I never realized, and I'm sure other people do not realize, how things are until they have a loved one on Medicaid/Medicare in a facility that provides only the basic of needs.

We tried to settle in as easily and comfortably as possible. Another bed was brought in for me, because they realized I was also there to stay. Ray and I fell into a routine where we got up at 7:00 a.m. After I had begged for coffee for a few months from the physical therapy room, I purchased a coffee maker and Ray and I had a cup together every morning. After a short time, staff members would also come for a cup. One morning I made twenty-three cups of coffee! While the coffee was brewing, I set up his breathing apparatus so he could have a treatment. He really enjoyed his breakfast, which began with fruit, such as pineapple, melon, strawberries, blueberries, raspberries, and watermelon. After this he had yogurt, avocado, or cereal. These were the foods I bought. Sometimes the facility offered bacon or sausages, which are two of his favorite breakfast treats. I shopped every week and filled up our little refrigerator with enough good food to last until the next shopping day. We quickly learned that the food served in the facility was not appealing, especially to Ray, who was used to cooking fine foods. Occasionally, family members or friends would bring him food. Two friends in particular who enjoy cooking, Carol and Stan, had brought us several meals while we were at the rehabilitation facility, and they also brought us good home-cooked meals here too. Those were the most delicious meals we had, and we really looked forward to them.

I would leave around nine, sometimes driving home in tears because I had to leave him and go to my house, which didn't even feel like a home anymore. Even my parents didn't understand when I would complain to them. They had no idea the heartache I was going through most days. They just kept telling me I needed to sleep at home instead of being with Ray every night. That broke my heart.

They didn't understand how much this had changed his life as well as mine, and that he'd been hurt in such a way that even I didn't always understand how he felt. However, I wanted him to know that I'd always be there for him. I believe this was the only thing that kept him going then, to know that he could always count on me. So many times I said to him, "We're in this alone. You and me against the world." Often I wished I could make people understand how much we needed their support and not their advice.

It took about three months to deplete our funds for the spend-down and I was told exactly how to do it. I had to get rid of Ray's 2000 Saab and my 1999 Grand Am and buy an expensive new vehicle. I went to a couple of dealerships with my brother Dick, and I decided on a 2005 Chevrolet Uplander for $39,000. It stated on the window sticker that the Uplander could be transformed into a handicap accessible vehicle. However, after I purchased it, I went to a garage that specialized in handicapped vehicles and was told it couldn't be done with the accessorizing I needed. That presented a problem because, not only did I own a seven-passenger vehicle, I still needed a handicapped van!

I was able to keep our home, which was now in my name only, and my new car, which I wasn't crazy about, especially now that I was stuck with it not serving the purpose it was intended for. However, I still had quite a bit of money to spend. I put over $100,000 into the principal of my mortgage, which my attorney suggested, saying it was one way to "save" some of the money I had to spend. It also left me with a low monthly mortgage payment, which I could easily afford. Since Ray had a closet full of jeans he couldn't wear anymore, I spent a portion of the money on comfortable clothes for him. This included several pairs of sweatpants, which in the past he would never wear outside of our home. He was strictly a jeans-and-T-shirt guy. He couldn't wear his cowboy boots anymore, either. Now it was only sneakers, moccasins, or slippers. Before the accident, whenever he got dressed up he wore jeans, a sports jacket, and cowboy boots, and always looked so handsome.

I asked my attorney if I could give my daughter a significant amount of money; she told me that was definitely out of the question.

No gifts could be given and that would be considered a gift. I felt bad about that and have often thought that I should have found a way. I know how it is to struggle when you're young, although my daughter seemed to be doing just fine. However, money is always a good thing to have, and it would have made more sense to me than to spend it on something I didn't need or want.

In March 2005, Ray finally got a loaner motorized wheelchair, and the nurse told me it was the most fun they'd had at the nursing home in years. He was crashing into walls and almost ran over a nurse who had to jump out of the way. They finally took the chairs out of the chapel and let him practice in there. He really loved being able to move by himself. It was his first source of independence. The second day he was in it for about fifteen minutes and it just stopped. Of course, no one knew why. That same day his voice-activated phone stopped working and was packed up and sent to be repaired.

Late one night during the first year, when his temperature reached 101 and even Tylenol didn't help, the nurse thought he should have the special antibiotic injection that was kept on hand for him for situations such as this. The injection had been used only once before. He was prone to urinary tract infections because of his Foley catheter, and his temperature could rise rapidly. She asked for my opinion, and I agreed. When she came into the room with the medication, I noticed that she had four vials, when in the past there had been only two. I was hesitant about her using all four, even though she explained that four small ones contained the same amount as the two larger ones that had been used previously. This meant he would get two shots in each hip instead of one. Still concerned, I asked if it could harm him if he was given too much. She assured me that it wouldn't, but then said, "It's your call." With the needle in her hand, and the feeling in my heart that he was not going to improve without the medicine, I gave her permission to inject him. Then I watched over him for three long hours to make sure he didn't lapse into a coma—or worse—because of my decision. Luckily, his temperature started to drop so I was able to get a couple hours of much needed sleep. It turned out to be another urinary tract infection, but it could have been a lot worse if the medication was not available.

The next time I saw Gina was for her thirtieth birthday celebration in April 2005. I went to Minneapolis for the weekend and brought my friend Samanthia. I knew she would be a great traveling companion, and she and Gina were becoming fast friends.

The weather cooperated, remaining unseasonably in the eighties throughout the entire time. We went to the Mall of America during the day and partied at night. Several friends of Gina's also traveled to Minneapolis for her birthday, which made it extra special. On Sunday, April 10, which was her actual birthday, we all went to brunch, where I made a toast and thanked all of her friends for coming so far for this momentous occasion.

I knew it would be too difficult to say good-bye the next morning, so I went straight to the airport with Samanthia without seeing her.

On Saturday, April 29, Ray experienced excruciating neck pain that he could hardly tolerate. By the next morning, he had chills and a low-grade fever. Sunday night he hallucinated all night long, and on Monday morning he had a temperature of 103.2. He was taken to the hospital emergency room, where they drew blood, tested his urine, and administered a chest X-ray. He remained in the emergency room until the wee hours of the morning on Tuesday, when he was finally taken to a room for a stay of five days with a urinary tract infection. During the rare times that his body temperature was that high, he tended to have strange dreams. On this occasion, he said he and Bill, my former husband, were each placed on barbecue spits by some strange looking people who wanted to make sausages out of them. First they were going to cut off their arms and legs with a chain saw and feed them to the dogs. Bill's sister, Mary, happened to get there in time to stop them.

On May 16 Ray was awake most of the night with congestion, so we went to the hospital early the next morning. His chest X-ray was negative for pneumonia, and the blood tests did not show an infection. He was given a breathing treatment and sent back to the nursing home.

At approximately 9:00 pm. on Saturday, June 4, when I got there after work, his drainage bag was full of blood, he was running a temperature, and was nauseous. We went to the hospital and, as usual, blood was drawn, a urine sample was taken, and a chest X-ray was taken. It was determined that he had another urinary tract infection. An intravenous antibiotic was administered, and three hours later he was returning to the nursing home. All day Sunday he was freezing, even though the outside temperature was around ninety degrees. I piled the blankets on him, but then his temperature started rising. The drainage bag was once again filling with blood and his temperature reached 102. He started hallucinating and had another crazy dream that he was swimming in a bowl of Campbell's soup and all the noodles were after him, wearing helmets and carrying guns! The fire alarm went off, which was a false alarm, but brought the local fire trucks to the scene. The commotion was right outside his second-story window, and he seemed afraid of the noise and couldn't really understand what was happening. He was trying to talk to me but his speech was jumbled. The nurse gave him a Xanax to try to calm him down and called his regular doctor. He ordered the special antibiotic once again, because his temperature had gone beyond the 101 mark. Thankfully it helped, and each day he felt a little better.

It took several months for me to reach the spend-down goal of $92,000 that was set by the state. On June 10, 2005, I received a call from my attorney informing me that Ray had finally been accepted for Title 19, which would be retroactive back to February. She said I should receiving confirmation in the mail soon, which I received the next day. Out of the money he would receive from the state, the facility would get all but $60, which was all he would have to spend every month. We decided that the Medicaid funds be deposited directly into my checking account, and I would make out a check to the facility each month.

That same month the photographer from the local newspaper called, asking if he could visit in the early afternoon. I told him we were going to have our hair done by our personal hairdresser, who came to the facility, and he asked if he could photograph that and do a short story for the newspaper. We told him it was all right as long as our hairdresser had no objections. Kim was a traveling hairdresser and had been cutting Ray's hair in our home for many years. It was convenient to have mine done at the facility too, so she had become my personal hairdresser as well. The photographer had taken our pictures several times in the past, and we were becoming friends. He enjoyed Ray's company and visited occasionally. The article was interesting—it showed her coloring my hair!

On Tuesday, June 28, Ray ran a temperature all day, so I stayed by his bedside trying to make him comfortable. He was scheduled for a body massage, and I didn't want to cancel it because I thought it might help him feel better. However, a short time after the massage his temperature was still pretty high, and I put wet cloths on his head to try to lower it. A nurse called the doctor, and he ordered the famous standby antibiotic.

After the injection, his temperature dropped to100.9 during the night, but by the next morning it shot up to 102. The nurse put ice packs under his arms while waiting for the doctor's call. The temperature started to drop again, but the doctor wanted him to go to the hospital so they could monitor him closely. Ray was admitted and given an intravenous antibiotic, along with the standard blood and urine tests and chest X-ray. Again he had a urinary tract infection!

He spent the next two days in the hospital. This time was different. He seemed sicker than the previous hospitalizations, and I was getting nervous. I knew he was scared when he said to me that he would wait for me "up there," and he would find his mother and father and a nice vehicle to go riding in. That saddened me, and I told him he couldn't leave me yet because we still had too many things to do! He made it through that scary ordeal and left the hospital on July 1.

On Thursday morning July 28, after an uncomfortable night, he woke with chills and a temperature of 101. We both knew that this was the beginning of another urinary tract infection, so it was back to the hospital. Of course, it was the same routine with the blood, urine, and chest X-ray. He was also given liquid Motrin, which helped relax his sore back muscles. After nine long hours in the emergency room, he was admitted and transferred to the third floor where he remained for several days.

His customized, motorized wheelchair arrived on August 8. It was a highly technical machine, and he spent all afternoon trying to learn how to move it with his chin. After several days, he decided it would be easier to manipulate with his mouth because his beard, which had grown back, was making his chin slip off the knob. The chair also reclined, and at times he seemed to be practically lying down with his feet in the air. He had constant blood pressure issues and knew when he needed to recline, which would raise his pressure. And if his blood pressure got too high, he could sit completely upright, which would lower it.

One Friday evening I called the facility at 7:00 p.m. to see if everything was all right. I hadn't heard from him all day long, which was unusual. The nurse supervisor answered the phone and said Ray was fine and that he was sitting right by the desk. I asked if they could give him his shower soon because our friends, Judy and Joe, come faithfully every Friday night about 7:45, and he really looked forward to their visits. When I arrived after work around nine, Ray informed me that they had started getting him ready after seven thirty, and Judy and Joe had had to wait thirty minutes. I asked the nurse if they could try to get him ready earlier in the future. Her response was, "Perhaps you could ask your guests to come a little later." Had they forgotten about "residents' rights"?

There was quite a commotion one Monday in October when Ray was getting ready for his shower. The shower chair that was used by only two residents in the whole facility was being used by the other resident at that same time. I knew we were going to have to change this situation, so I went to a supervisor and explained the problem. She decided to change Ray's Monday shower from morning to evening.

"The night shift isn't going to like that," I said. She said she didn't care.

When that shift found out about it, they were furious. The shower ordeal wasn't pleasant for him either, because the transfer from the bed to the shower chair via a Hoyer Lift was more than he wanted to endure. After that he decided to have a shower only once a week.

One night, shortly after he fell asleep, he woke up yelling, "Help me!"

I ran to his bedside to see what was wrong. He told me his mother and father had come to get him, but he told them he wasn't ready yet. They said they would be back another time to take him. As I bent down to comfort him, he said, "You're leaning on my father. Can't you see him?" A few nights later, he yelled for help and told me they were back. He asked me to grab his feet so they couldn't take him away.

We had a care-plan meeting in mid-October and were told that Ray was eligible for fifty-eight hours of home care. He was entitled to a special air mattress, a Hoyer Lift, and a shower chair. A Hoyer Lift is a transfer device that Ray needs because he can't move. A special piece of fabric called a Hoyer pad is placed under him and is attached to a series of hooks. The pad holds Ray in place while he is lifted from the bed to the chair. I was told I could get a grant to renovate our bathroom to accommodate Ray's needs. What I was not told at that time was that a lien would be put on my home for ten years, and each year 10 percent of the lien would drop off. There was no way that was going to happen! I asked if Ray could come home and take only bed baths. The answer was yes, so it was settled. No bathroom renovation. We were given a release date of February 14, 2006—Valentine's Day!

Gina called one evening in late 2005 with exciting news: she was going to be in a movie. She and a girlfriend, who had taken a few community tap dance classes, had combined their love for the local music scene with their dancing, and had recruited another friend who did much of their choreography. The three of them took to the stage in their tap shoes and became the Shim Sham Shufflers. They opened for some local bands and performed at various benefits in the Twin Cities. One of the casting directors heard about them from a radio contact, pulled their pictures from MySpace, liked their look, and asked them to come in for an audition. They shot two different scenes but didn't know how much of a presence they would have. However, it was a totally amazing experience for Gina, especially meeting actor John C. Reilly. The movie, *A Prairie Home Companion*, is about the last performance of a radio show that has been on the air for many years. She also met well-known producers, directors, actors, and actresses, such as Meryl Streep, Lily Tomlin, Woody Harrelson, and Lindsey Lohan. I was so excited. Gina was talented in the arts, and ever since she went to modeling school in her senior year of high school I had a dream of her being destined for "something big." She said the release date for the movie was April 2006.

She had spent the previous two Christmases in Connecticut with us, and decided she wanted to remain in Minneapolis for Christmas 2005, but came home for Thanksgiving. There were always so many friends and family members for her to see, and she set aside special time to spend with Ray. One evening she brought him sushi and, since he had no other visitors, they were able to spend time alone. This touched my heart, and I could tell it made him very happy too.

Many times I e-mailed her when I was stressed or depressed, even though I didn't want to upset her. She was one of the few that I thought understood.

On Monday evening, December 12, Ray was scheduled for his weekly shower. I went to get the shower chair and noticed it was broken. The first time he had realized it was broken was in August, and I had told the supervisor that I'd like it fixed before he was scheduled to use it again. However, on the night of December 12, Ray was Hoyered into the chair and wheeled into the tiny shower room at approximately 7:30. I washed his hair and beard while the aide bathed his body. When it was time to rinse him off, we pulled him forward so we could rinse his back. The footrest gave way and he landed on the floor with his right arm lodged between the seat and the arm of the chair. The aide pulled the emergency cord, and I ran out into the hallway to find some help. Not a single person was within sight!

I ran downstairs to try to find someone. In the meantime, Suzanne, the LPN on duty who was, thankfully, a great nurse, came to the rescue with several helpers. While I waited outside the shower room, they placed a sheet blanket under Ray's body and everyone lifted him onto the chair. Then they did the same from the chair to the bed. The nurse examined his body and told us that there were no cuts on his skin, but he had a bright red bruise under his right shoulder. She ordered portable X-rays, which were taken about 10:00 pm, and they revealed a fractured bone in his wrist. Of course he couldn't feel it, but it was swollen so he knew there was damage.

"It's too bad you don't have your camera with you," he said to me.

He didn't realize I carried most of my possessions with me, rather than leave them at home. Unfortunately, when I tried to use my camera, I discovered the battery was dead. Then I realized my cell phone had a camera. I took a few pictures of the shower chair, but it had been taken outside so the pictures were very dark. I went looking for it early the next morning, but it was nowhere in sight so I never got any good pictures.

Shortly after that, Ray was admitted to the hospital for one of his frequent urinary tract infections. By the time he returned, he was scheduled for his weekly shower. I asked about the shower chair and was told the replaceable parts have not come in yet. I went to the administrator and told her that Ray has not had a shower for over three weeks! Miraculously, the chair was fixed and Ray was able to have his shower.

On Friday, December 23, Ray was not feeling well at all. His blood pressure was erratic and he was experiencing chills. In the early evening, his eyes started rolling, and I thought he was going to pass out as his blood pressure dipped. The supervisor came in and gently slapped his face several times, telling him to "stay with us." She called the doctor, who said to make sure he drank plenty of liquids and to keep a close eye on him for a few hours. Luckily, he was able to have his usual Friday night visitors. They had phoned several times and were concerned about his situation that evening, because they wanted to present me with Ray's Christmas gift to me:

Opium perfume, which was one of my favorites. I was so surprised they had arranged this without my knowledge because Ray has not been good about keeping secrets from me in the past.

During the night, he knew his blood pressure had dropped. Thinking I was asleep, he asked the nurse to move his legs, which helps to raise the pressure, but she had no idea what to do! I told her to leave the room and I would take care of it. After a few minutes, his blood pressure rose and he felt better.

The next day was Christmas Eve. He was still not feeling well, so I was hesitant about going home to shower and change. Instead, I stayed, even though I'd worn the same clothes all the previous day and all night long as well. This was a familiar situation which had happened in the past when he'd gotten sick unexpectedly.

We had several visitors that day, who all appeared at approximately the same time in that small room. It was a little overwhelming being so crowded, especially with Ray not feeling well. We knew that another infection was brewing because he had all the symptoms, and we thought we could make it through the holiday without his being hospitalized. It was also depressing. Christmas Eve was our favorite day of the year, and after having spent it in the rehabilitation facility last year, we were hoping to get home this year for a few hours with the family. It wasn't to be because there was no transportation! By the end of the day I was so depressed, thinking of the Christmas Eves in the past.

Christmas Day 2005 I had to work—thank goodness. I could leave that suffocating place and finally go home and take a shower. I didn't know how Ray stood it for twenty-four hours a day every single day without complaining. He had no visitors on Christmas until about nine that night, when my niece Dina brought him the remainder of her Christmas dinner.

Ray was admitted to the hospital on January 1, 2006, for the usual urinary tract infection, and he remained for eight days. We thought what a lousy way to begin the New Year!

After we had been at the facility for about fifteen months, things started to change within the staff. We heard about employees calling out sick, and at times it seemed there weren't enough people working to take care of the residents' needs. I witnessed a staff member tell an elderly lady in tears to stop crying. One evening a resident told a nurse her glasses were dirty and tried to hand them to her to clean but the nurse said she was busy. I overheard another nurse tell a resident to go to his room. In the past, I hadn't been overly fond of old people, but I soon realized how their lives changed when they were put in a nursing home until the day they died sometimes never seeing the outside world again, or even anyone from that world. We were more fortunate than most … we had each other.

Not all of our time at the facility was unpleasant. We made friends with members of the staff and with a few families that came to visit their loved ones. I liked being around people and there was always someone to talk to. One of the elderly residents had been there a short time when we became friendly with his children, who were slightly younger than us. We looked forward to their visits, and they always made sure they included spending time with us as well as their father. In fact, when I was in Minnesota visiting my daughter, they had a family picnic and included Ray. One son teamed up with the mayor of our town to launch a fund-raiser so we could finally get the much needed handicapped van.

One night when I got to the facility after work, one of the elderly man's daughters was in Ray's room. She told me that her dad had just passed away. It was a sad time, for they were the most devoted family I had ever known, and the support they gave their dad was out of love, not obligation. I immediately went to the dad's room, where I found them all sitting around the bed where their father, or grandfather, or father-in-law still lay, with his signature Red Sox ball cap on. Days later they presented us with a coffee cake and flowers in appreciation of the attention we gave their father.

Gina came home again to celebrate her thirty-first birthday in April and spent time with Ray on a couple of different occasions. I went out to dinner with her on her birthday, and she was disappointed that Ray did not come. I explained that it would be difficult for him, because when he had a blood pressure issue, he tilted his wheelchair back to an almost upside-down position, which would not be feasible in a restaurant. Her dad and his wife joined us and we had a very pleasant dinner.

In July 2006, Ray was scheduled for a follow-up appointment at the neurologist for his shoulder pain. He was planning on going in the wheelchair instead of a stretcher, as the doctor had suggested. The wheelchair ambulance came to transport him, and a staff member told him the wheelchair wouldn't fit in the vehicle so he was unable to keep an appointment that was very important to him because of his constant shoulder discomfort. He tried to tell them that he had been in the vehicle before, but no one listened. Unfortunately, the person who scheduled appointments such as this was absent that day. She would have taken charge of the situation and he would have been able to keep the appointment.

From July 2005 through July 2006, Ray was admitted to the hospital ten times. Except for two cases of pneumonia, all of the incidents were urinary tract infections. The first few days in the hospital would seem like a little vacation for him, but then it became routine and he would get restless and want to be back in the familiar territory of the facility, which would also enable him to get out of bed and into his wheelchair.

On August 2, 2006, while in the hospital for another slight urinary tract infection and congestion in his chest that was classified as pneumonia, he had an operation called a suprapubic catherization. This is done by inserting a thin tube through the skin just above the pubic bone into the bladder. It's a common treatment used among spinal cord injury patients who are unable to use intermittent catherization to empty the bladder. The operation took about twenty minutes and the recovery time was an hour and a half, while the nurses tried to raise his body temperature. He seemed to be okay when he came back to his room. This was also our nineteenth wedding anniversary, and when I arrived at the hospital that morning, I found a dozen yellow roses and a beautiful card from him, compliments of a friend. What a wonderful surprise! He was so proud that he'd been able to recognize our special day with our favorite flower, and I made sure I let him know how much I appreciated it. The previous year he also had been in the hospital for our anniversary. I told him it was all right and that we would make up for it in the future.

After he was released from the hospital, the suprapubic catheter didn't seem to be doing what it was supposed to do. It wasn't draining properly, so another catheter was inserted in the penis as before. Now he had two drainage bags! This was defeating the purpose of the suprapubic catheter. This continued for almost two weeks, and on August 14, 2006, he was taken to the emergency room on the doctor's request. The suprapubic catheter was removed and he was right back where he started with the original catheter.

Just before this operation, his blood pressure had started to level out. After the suprapubic catheter was removed, it was erratic again for about six weeks.

After he got out of the hospital, I called the company that serviced his wheelchair and told them the boom on the chair needed to be adjusted. The man I spoke with told me there needed to be an "in-service" on the chair because every person dealing with Ray has to know how to position him in the chair so he's in direct line with the lever he uses with his mouth to move the chair..It's not the property of the facility, but a personal wheelchair that belongs to Ray. If someone doesn't know how to work it, especially the mouthpiece that he steers with, he's unable to use the chair until that part gets fixed, which means he's confined to bed during that time. If physical therapy could not do an in-service, the man said he would come and do it. The night before, an aide didn't know how to work the mouthpiece and had attempted to pull it the wrong way until Ray yelled for her to stop.

Gina came home again in August for her friend's thirtieth birthday. She spent a few hours with us when she first arrived before meeting friends. She kept busy as usual, visiting friends and family, and before we knew it, it was time for me to take her to the airport for another teary good-bye.

One night in the middle of August, when it was time for Ray to get ready for bed, I noticed that his air mattress had deflated. The motor for the bed had not worked for two days, which I had reported to management. Here we were two days later and he was still on the same mattress, slowly losing air by the hour, instead of on a replacement mattress. Of course I raised a little hell like I usually do when something went wrong, and asked the nurses what they were going to do to rectify the situation. They said he might have to sleep on a regular mattress that night and get the correct one in the morning. I told them it would be okay if they were sure they could make that happen. He absolutely had to have an air mattress because of the bedsore issue. Well, lo and behold, a few minutes later an air mattress appeared out of nowhere!

The morning of August 27, Ray woke up at 6:15 and realized he had not been turned at 5:00, as he was scheduled. Since it only takes two hours for a bedsore to form, being turned on time is very important. When he blew on his call bell and the aides came in to reposition him, they asked if he had had the chicken salad for dinner. He said, no, he didn't eat that crap. They told him it was a good thing because there had been many sick people during the night. That was why they hadn't turned him. However, the next day we were told an intestinal virus was spreading through the facility, and signs were posted at all the entrances to discourage visitors until the epidemic passed. One of the nurses told me to make sure I washed my hands whenever I touched something so I didn't get sick. She said that even the outside community was getting sick, so it couldn't be the food. Ray and I thought differently.

One day in September, I noticed that two of Ray's toes were black and blue, and I asked him what had happened. He said it must have been when they got jammed by the Hoyer Lift as he was being lifted out of his chair and into bed. He said sometimes they were in a hurry to get him into bed as fast as humanly possible. The nurse thought the toes should be X-rayed. Luckily, they were not broken, just badly bruised. One night he said to me, "If I die while I'm in here, make sure you have an autopsy done."

Another incident in September was the scabies prevention episode. We had already been through one the year before when there was an outbreak. Each resident's family received a letter from the facility stating that they were taking precautions before an outbreak occurred. The procedure was to rub cream, from neck to toes, on all one hundred twenty residents. Sixty residents on Sunday night and the remaining sixty on Monday night. The follow morning, the residents got showers to wash off the cream. All the bed linens were washed, as well as each resident's entire wardrobe. The rooms were thoroughly cleaned, as well as the rugs, furniture, wheelchairs, walkers, and canes. The residents were asked to stay in their rooms and wear hospital johnnies until their clothes were returned to them. Since I did Ray's laundry, I took everything out of his room during that time. Ray was "creamed" on Monday night and was the last one to get a shower on Tuesday morning. When I left at 9:30 a.m., there were eleven residents sitting in their wheelchairs, waiting in line for a shower! Before I could retrieve our own pillows to take home to clean or destroy, the facility took them out to wash with the other residents' possessions, and we lost four good pillows that were never returned.

Ray went back to see the neurologist on September 20, which was his third attempt for a follow-up visit for the shoulder pain. The doctor gave him a prescription for twice a day range-of-motion and perhaps a visit to the pain clinic. Because he's not scheduled for range-of-motion, a doctor has to prescribe it in order for it to be effective. The nurse told him not to refuse pain medication if his pain is chronic. She said that, with his condition, he would need new and different medications all his life.

Only certain aides will do range-of-motion exercises without complaining. In August 2007, Ray asked an aide to please move his legs because he could tell his blood pressure was dropping. Some of the aides didn't understand how much range-of-motion helped to bring up his blood pressure. This aide said she had done it once and it had hurt her back, so she was not going to do it again.

Gina came for a short visit in October 2007. She and I had dinner at her favorite restaurant, which had become a tradition each time she came home. The next day I took her to have a manicure and pedicure from Paula, who had been doing mine for twenty years and had become one of my best friends and confidants during my darkest days. When it was time to drive Gina to the airport, I gave her a book that I had been working on for several months about "my legacy." She called me a few days later and said she read the book on the plane and loved it. However, she didn't realize how much her move to Minneapolis had affected me.

One day Ericka, a friend and coworker of mine, came to visit us and brought her three-year-old daughter Christyna. She kept staring at Ray's wheelchair. He thought she was afraid of it, but actually, she was just curious. I explained that he had fallen in the kitchen and that his arms, legs, and back were broken and didn't work anymore. She wanted to know how Ray got out of his chair and into the bed. I told her he was lifted out of the chair and lowered into the bed with a devise that looked like a sling, called a Hoyer.

Ericka told me later about her conversation with Christyna on their ride home. Ericka asked her daughter if she was afraid of Ray. When Christyna said no, Ericka asked why she'd been staring at Ray. The little girl said, "I know his arms, legs, and back are broken, but his head isn't broken and he can still say yes and no, right?" Ericka assured her that he could still say yes and no. Her next question was, "Is Ray's brain broken?" When Ericka said no, she asked if Ray's heart got broken. Again Ericka said, "No, Ray's heart is not broken." The three year old thought for a minute and then stated, "If he can still say yes and no and his brain isn't broken and his heart isn't broken, then Ray will be okay!"

Out of the mouth of babes!

On March 3, 2007, Ray wasn't feeling well in the morning so he decided to remain in bed a little longer than usual. When he told the aide that, she said, "If you don't get up now, you're not getting up." He felt better after lunch, so about 1:30 he told the aide he would like to get up. She said, "I'm going to make believe I didn't hear that. You can wait for the next shift now."

This is an example of someone who doesn't care about the people she's supposed to be helping, and about Ray being so dependent on someone who just plain doesn't give a damn. Again, what about Residents Rights?

As the 2007 year was ending, it was discovered that Ray had a sore on the heel of his left foot. Many months earlier I had bought a foot massager that I thought would be good for the circulation in his legs. We used it every night after he was in bed. We both thought the sore had been caused by his feet rubbing against each other. It was measured periodically and treated twice every day until it disappeared. I took the foot massager home and never used it again.

A little while after that, we invested in Venodynes, which are inflatable cuffs that fit over the calves of the legs to help circulation, which was especially important in Ray's situation since he couldn't move his legs. The cuffs are compressed by a motor that is attached to each cuff by a tube. The Venodynes were put on when he went to bed and taken off when he woke up. The girl in the insurance office said that with a prescription for Venodynes, Medicare might reimburse us. We called Ray's doctor, who presented us with the prescription, the girl sent it to Medicare along with the purchase receipt, and Medicare paid us $1300!

On March 27, 2008, Ray was running a temp of 100.2, which was high for him because his normal body temperature was 96. He knew this was a sign of an impending urinary tract infection. By this time he had become quite knowledgeable in the precautions he needed to take in order to prevent a hospital visit. He told the acting nursing director that the catheter needed to be changed. She said they normally hesitated doing that because it could breed infection. Ray said he knew that, but if it wasn't changed *he* would become infected. She said she had to check the records to see when it had been done last because she was not going to rely on his word. She also said that they would get a urine sample to send to the lab. After examining the records, she said the supervisor would be in to change it. That was at nine in the morning. She finally came in around four in the afternoon after a phone call from me!

The following morning, after the 5:00 a.m. turning, I noticed the catheter tube was wrapped around Ray's leg and he was lying on the drainage bag. To us, this was carelessness. The next night, at 11:00 p.m., 2:00 a.m., and 5:00 a.m., his bed had to be completely changed, as well as his night shirt, because urine was leaking from the catheter. The nurse labeled the problem as "positional." In the morning, a different nurse noticed that the catheter had pulled about three inches out of the penis. Again it had to be reinserted. The end result was a three-day trip to the hospital with a urinary tract infection! We both felt that this was because the facility was not acting in Ray's best interest. A urine sample was never taken.

During the first week of April 2008, I made a couple of calls to see if Ray was eligible for a group home. I quickly learned that if he had a brain injury he would be. That not being the case, his only option was to remain in the "skilled nursing facility" that he had called home for the last three and a half years.

On the evening of April 14, 2008, Ray called me at work just before quitting time to inform me that he wasn't feeling well and that the doctor had been called. He said he felt "funny," as he usually did with the onset of an infection. Also, his oral antibiotic that he took four times a day to help control urinary infections had been depleted and had not been replaced for several doses.

The doctor called and ordered an antibiotic at night, which arrived at nine the next morning! Unfortunately, this resulted in a two-day trip to the hospital for another infection.

In September 2008, Ray had another suprapubic operation because his penis had become so traumatized during the past four years. After his hospital stay, he returned for another eight days when the catheter tube was accidentally pulled out and had to be reinserted. He ended the year with another overnight stay at the hospital, this time with cellulitis, which is a potentially serious bacterial skin infection.

After that, there were so many changes at the facility. The aides were all switched around, put on different wings and different floors, and Ray, for one, was very upset. For three years he'd had the same aides. They knew how to take care of him and knew the mechanics of his personalized wheelchair, which was an important concern of his. However, the administration thought that placing the aides on different wings gave them a chance to get to know all the residents and their needs. They just didn't realize how much of an imposition this was on the residents. This was their home, whether temporary or permanent, and we thought they should have been considered in this decision. Also, Alzheimer patients do not like change. They tend to be afraid if they see a different face after they've become familiar and trusting with certain people.

I was able to take a much needed long weekend and visit my daughter for my sixty-fourth birthday, and arrived in Minneapolis on Friday, December 5, 2008. Gina picked me up at the airport and drove me to my motel in the falling snow. After I checked in and dropped off my luggage, we drove to her house where I met her roommate, whom I liked instantly. Shortly after, she and several of her friends took me to a wonderful Italian restaurant for my birthday dinner. The snow was still falling during our meal, but had tapered off by the time we left. Gina hates the cold weather and also does not like driving in the snow, so she probably would have avoided going out that night had I not been there.

The next day, since Gina was a vegan at the time, we went to a "raw" restaurant for lunch. She informed me that the food was served cold. Nothing was cooked. I decided on salad and juice, which was surprisingly good. I walked through the rooms of the restaurant, which was situated in a house, and noticed they sold juicers. Remembering Gina wanted one, I asked what her preference was. She advised me not to buy one because I was going to get her a laptop for Christmas. Disregarding her advice, I bought one, which made her very happy—and I love it when she's happy!

Our next stop was downtown Minneapolis, because she wanted to purchase tickets at a box office for a show in January. We parked the car and walked a couple of blocks on that cold and windy Minnesota day. She took me to an art museum in the late afternoon and then to her house, where she cooked us a dinner consisting of mashed potatoes, carrots, and tofu. I could tell she enjoyed cooking. Plus, it was very good! She was excited as she unpacked and assembled her new juicer, and I knew it had been well worth the money. She took me back to my motel about ten when she was on her way to work, bartending a special party.

The next day we went to brunch with several of her friends, which was a weekly event for them. After brunch we went to The Mall of America to purchase the laptop computer I was giving her for Christmas. We went back to the motel and she "played" on the computer for several hours, transferring pictures from her camera to the computer and showed them via a slide show. She also transferred videos that she and her friends made and gave me a CD/DVD for my computer. We spent a lot of time together, and before I knew it, it was Monday morning and she had to take me to the airport where, as usual, I bid a teary good-bye. Every time I left her I was still very sad, because I never knew when I would see her again.

In January 2009, Ray was back at the hospital for three days with a urinary tract infection and cellulitis. Since he was getting cellulitis so often and had to be hospitalized needing an IV antibiotic, the doctor decided to insert a PICC line in his arm so he could have the IV given at the nursing home. A PICC line is a form of <u>intravenous</u> access that can be used for a prolonged period of time. A long, thin, flexible catheter is inserted into one of the large veins of the arm near the bend of the elbow. It is then slid into the vein until the tip of the catheter sits in a large vein just above the heart.

In February, one of our favorite nurses passed away. Actually, she had been the first nurse assigned to Ray when he arrived at the facility over three years earlier. When we approached her several months ago about her noticeable weight loss, she confessed how she hadn't eaten in several days because her stomach was always upset and she thought she might have an ulcer. The last day she worked, she said she had an appointment with the doctor the next day, and Ray said to me, "I have a feeling she won't be back." Unfortunately, he was right. After many tests that diagnosed cancer and a trip to another doctor for a second opinion on treatment options, she passed away four months later. It was a sad time at the nursing home. I had spoken to her when she was first hospitalized. She was feeling better and seemed positive that she would recover from whatever was ailing her. Unfortunately, the facility lost one of their best nurses. She had even taken care of me for a couple of days when I had a stomach virus and had to remain at the facility because I was too sick to leave and didn't want to be home alone. She made sure I drank plenty of ginger ale so I wouldn't become dehydrated and helped me to the bathroom whenever necessary.

Another nurse I had also become friendly with lost her life. She fell on the ice one winter night while getting in her car to come to work, and had to be taken to the hospital in an ambulance. While being operated on for a broken leg, she had complications due to her weight and a respiratory condition, and after a few weeks she had a seizure and eventually passed away.

All during 2009, Ray's body was infected approximately six times with cellulitis, seven times with urinary infections, along with continuing blood pressure issues and congestion.

The following year, 2010, began with changing the suprapubic catheter. One day he had a temperature of 101, and he knew it was the beginning of another urinary tract infection. The antibiotic could now be administered at the facility through the PICC line, so a hospital trip was avoided. In March the PICC line was removed from his left arm, since it had been in for a little over a year, and another was inserted in his right arm. It was working well, eliminating his hospital visits and enabling him to be treated with the antibiotics at the nursing home. The antibiotics were usually for seven days, every twelve hours. He was constantly doing breathing treatments to eliminate the congestion and ease his breathing. Whenever he went to the hospital, they checked his blood, urine, and lungs because of his compromised immune system.

The morning of March 22, he was sent to the emergency room for congestion, which proved positive for pneumonia. A contraption known as a vibrating vest was wrapped around his chest. When it was turned on, it shook him so hard, the congestion was loosened and he was able to breathe more easily. Temporarily. The procedure was repeated throughout his eight-day stay. One afternoon I received a call at work that his breathing had been in distress and a very expensive drug was needed. The nurse said it was a good thing I had excellent insurance because Medicare refused to pay for the drug. I slept in his hospital room that night because I was afraid he would have a problem breathing and the nurse wouldn't get to his room fast enough.

Along with that bout with pneumonia, that year the suprapubic was more troublesome than before. It needed to be irrigated and changed more because of low or no urine output. When a urinary catheter is not draining well, a procedure called irrigation is needed to "unplug" the catheter. Saline is inserted into the catheter with a syringe so that urine can drain from the bladder.

CHAPTER 5

‖‖‖

Under New Management

The only disability in life is a bad attitude.
Scott Hamilton

The atmosphere in the facility had changed drastically since that snowy January day Ray first arrived, with new owners and new management staff. Most of the time the floor staff consisted of two aides on the 3:00 p.m. to 11:00 p.m. shift, which made things difficult because it reduced the patient care. Some residents, like Ray, are a two-person assist, which meant he needed two aides whenever he was Hoyered into and out of bed. At times, that didn't always leave an aide on the wing in case another resident needed assistance.

In one incident, during this busy shift, the two aides were assisting Ray as he was being Hoyered into bed, and a resident wandered out the door and down the street. Someone finally recognized him and called the facility. The aide assigned to that resident was one of the two helping to get Ray in bed, and she was suspended because she had *allowed* the wandering resident to walk out of the facility. After her suspension, she quit. She was a good aide and had worked in the business for many years, and said she wasn't going to waste her time working in a facility that was unreasonable.

The morning of September 26, 2010, Ray's blood pressure was higher than was comfortable for him, so we knew something was brewing—another urinary tract infection. High blood pressure was always a sign that he should be closely monitored, but the only thing the morning nurse was interested in was passing out medication. When we told her of the situation, her reply was, "We'll keep our eye on it." Actually, *I* took his blood pressure, as I did every morning. She didn't bother to check for herself and left at three without apparently ever giving it another thought.

Luckily, the relief nurse was concerned and monitored Ray's blood pressure all during her shift. When I got there at 9:00, she told me she might have to send him to the hospital because his heart rate was also elevated. She assured us she would continue to monitor him since she would be working all through the night, even though she was on the adjacent wing.

As it turned out, we needed her assistance. The nurse assigned to Ray's wing came in the room at 5:00 a.m. to monitor his oxygen level, which he seldom had an issue with. I was very angry and practically yelled at her.

"He doesn't have a problem breathing," I said. "His blood pressure has been the issue for a whole day! Why weren't you thinking about that?"

She replied to Ray, "I'll be back to take your blood pressure."

When she finally took it, it was 165/101! He told her that was too high, and she asked what did *we* want to do about it? At that point, I got the other nurse, and she called for the ambulance to take him to the hospital. At 6:30 he was on his way for the short trip, and he was, naturally, diagnosed with a urinary tract infection. He was given an oral medication, which he would continue for five days, and returned to the facility at 9:30—with normal blood pressure!

Gina completely surprised me on Christmas Eve 2010. She called me about six in the evening as she usually did on Christmas Eve and asked if I was planning on visiting anyone. I told her I was staying with Ray and would look forward to a Christmas Eve when we could be together again. A couple of hours later, she arrived at the nursing home! What a wonderful surprise. It certainly made my Christmas special! She also surprised my family the next day by appearing for Christmas dinner at the assisted living facility where my parents resided. Everyone was glad to see her, especially her cousin Dina, whom she had spent her entire childhood with. Needless to say, her visit was enjoyed by many and, again, encouraged by her father, who had told her not to put the impending visit on Facebook because I would see it.

The evening of January 1, 2011, Ray arrived at the emergency room with a low grade temperature and low blood pressure. We were in the freezing cold emergency room for eight hours! Because we were so familiar with the emergency room and the long wait for test results, we always brought a couple of our own blankets. I know they have to keep it cool because of germs, but this area was frigid! They always have heated blankets, which Ray usually accepted along with his own blanket. I always dreaded going to the hospital because I knew what lay ahead each time, but he needed me. Without the use of his hands, he was unable to use a call bell. Plus, twice he had gone into anaphylactic shock from medication. One of those times he said he "saw the light" and thought he was dying, but he made it back to me.

Whenever he was admitted and taken to a room, they installed a device that connected to an adjustable tube that screwed onto his bed or table. When he blew into it, the light went on outside his room and at the nurse's station. It was the same system as the nursing home so he was familiar with it. However, in the emergency room he had no way to alert the staff if he was in distress, so I had to be with him during those times for the duration of his stay.

At 2:00 a.m., after the blood, urine, and chest X-ray results were finalized, he was admitted to the CCU because he was septic. Sepsis is a condition where the body is fighting a severe infection that has spread to the bloodstream.

He spent the first night of the New Year in the CCU and was transferred to a regular room the next day. I arrived around ten in the morning with his Kindle so he could pass the time reading.

He remained in the hospital until Friday, January 7, never receiving occupational therapy, physical therapy, or range of motion. The only movement he received was when I was present and ranged his arms and legs. He was supposed to be repositioned every two hours to prevent bed sores, and even though there was a clock outside his door as a reminder, *he* had to remind *them* several times. Twice his food tray sat for approximately an hour before someone came to feed him his then cold food! Hospitals and nursing homes should be made better aware of the care a person as dependent as Ray needs.

One very upsetting incident during this stay was when a nurse was preparing to irrigate his Foley catheter and used *tap* water. Since my husband and I were both familiar with the procedure, I questioned her about using either sterile water or saline, and she said that at this hospital, they used tap water. I was uneasy about this and should have stopped her, because in my heart I knew it was wrong. Later I approached another nurse, and she said they absolutely always used sterile water! I reported this to the charge nurse because, to us, this was a major error.

During his stay, the PICC line was replaced because it was the possible source of infection. An irregular heartbeat was detected, so he wore a heart monitor for twenty-four hours and then had an echocardiogram. He was put on Lasix for ten days because an X-ray had detected fluid around the lung. We were both thinking about the New Year and how it had begun, and wondered if this was a promise of what was to come. He was finally discharged on January 7 and sent back to the nursing home.

In February 2011, the bar Gina was working in closed, so she decided to travel by train to see friends in other states. I knew she had many friends, but never dreamed she had them in so many places! She left on Saturday, February 12, and arrived in Missoula, Montana, the next day. A few days later she was in Portland, Oregon. Her next stop was San Francisco and then on to Los Angeles. From there she went to Austin, Texas and New Orleans, where she spent a few days before arriving in Memphis, Tennessee. When she got to Chicago on March 11, she wasn't feeling well. Not much keeps her down though, so a couple of days later she was in Kansas City,

Kansas. She drove back to Austin with friends to attend a music festival. She decided to continue her journey, accompanying these same friends on their drive home. They continued on to Wichita, Kansas, where they spent the night before driving to Iowa City, Iowa. After a five and a half week excursion, she was back in Minneapolis on Wednesday, March 23.

On June 7, 2011, I sent an e-mail to the nursing home's ombudsman regarding patient safety. The ombudsman can be contacted if a resident or the resident's family feel that the resident's safety is at risk, which was exactly how we felt because of the staffing issue of the aides. He responded immediately and went to see Ray the following day. However, he basically told us that there was nothing he could do. Thanks!

During the summer of 2011, Ray was not able to enjoy the gazebo as he had in previous years, because it was packed full of unused wheelchairs that were usually stored elsewhere. The gazebo was open to the elements and the wheelchairs were there during the winter as well. The gazebo was intended for the residents' use, not for storage purposes. One evening in the beginning of 2012, when I arrived at the facility around nine, I saw a bed on the lawn by the ambulance entrance—equipped with a fitted sheet! It was wet because it had been there during the weekend of snow and rain. I guess if a homeless person needed a place to sleep, it was there and waiting!

Ray was in and out of the hospital a few more times for urinary infections, and in July he was hospitalized twice. The first time he had a kidney infection and an X-ray revealed a kidney stone. Of course, we had had no idea because of the paralysis. A drain was put in the kidney, and a few days later he was taken to the operating room for removal of the stone. I was waiting in his room when he returned and was told they were unsuccessful. When the urologist appeared, he explained that the stone was unreachable. So it was still there!

Ray returned to the hospital for a second time in July with very high blood pressure, a temperature of 102, and a high heart rate. When he got to the emergency room, his blood pressure took a nosedive, and the nurse would not leave his side until he was satisfied with the numbers. I was getting a little nervous because it seemed to take forever and I knew it was crucial. Finally, after a couple of hours, it reached a point where we knew he was going to be all right and I could breathe a sigh of relief. I praised that nurse and sent him a thank-you card, which was something I hadn't done in the past. I felt he was one in a million, and the hospital was lucky to have him on their staff.

During Ray's eight-day hospital stay, an X-ray revealed the stone had moved from the kidney to the bladder. He also had a urinary tract infection, as usual. When he was finally released, he had to continue taking an antibiotic at the nursing home via the PICC line four times a day for ten days.

The next time I saw Gina was in July 2011, when her grandmother, her dad's mom, passed away from Alzheimer's at eighty-eight years old. We attended the wake and funeral, where Gina was a pall bearer along with other grandchildren. She and I went out for dinner a couple of times, and before we knew it, it was time to say good-bye—again!

In August we were told that Ray had passed the kidney stone and would no longer have to worry about it. That surprised us, because we'd had no idea and neither had the staff. Nevertheless, it was good news. One less worry.

In September he suffered another urinary tract infection and was hospitalized for three days. He returned to the nursing home with the needed antibiotic for seven days.

My sister and I decided we needed to get away from the stress of our everyday lives, which were now compounded by my parents' failing health. Since my sister knew how much I wanted to see Gina, we were off to the Twin Cities. After arriving, we got our reserved rental car and drove to our motel. We got hopelessly lost though, and the thirty-minute drive took three hours. After we had checked in, we wanted to go to the bar where Gina was working as a mixologist—but we got lost again! Being very discouraged, we pulled over to the side of the road to relax for a moment, and right in front of us was the bar! We had made it!

It was a pleasure to see my little girl working in such a wonderful place, looking so professional. I was extremely proud of the woman she had become, and I could tell my sister was proud of her too. A few months earlier she had been one of four finalists in the Twin Cities' Most Inspired Bartender competition, where the mixologists competed each creating a new drink using Bombay Sapphire gin. Her picture had also been in the September issue of *Minnesota Monthly* magazine, standing behind her bar as she described one of the many exquisite drinks offered.

After a few eventful days, it was time for us to leave. How I wished we lived closer and could spend more time together. She lives a life that many envy, and I'm proud of the choices she's made and the unique woman she is today. She left Minnesota in mid-December 2011 and drove to her new home in Los Angeles with a girlfriend. I'm sure her stay in her new home state will be as rewarding as was her time spent in Minneapolis/St. Paul.

She and two friends got an apartment together, and she was able to guest bartend at an area bar. Things seemed to be working out in a timely manner. Shortly after, she was lucky enough to start bartending at a members-only club in West Hollywood, where she gets to see some famous actors and actresses.

In order to avoid bedsores, Ray sleeps on an air mattress. Since he had already experienced a wound from a bedsore, he was very cautious about his mattress. In December 2010, he noticed that it was not operating as it should and mentioned it to management. Nothing was done. One day a couple of months later, I got under the bed and noticed that a wire had become loose. As soon as I tightened it, the mattress began pumping as it should. However, a short time later it stopped again, and again we notified management. Time went by, we heard nothing, and were really getting frustrated.

One morning I happened to see the director and asked if anything was being done about the bed. She said, "There are other matters to contend with beside Ray's bed."

To us, this was an urgent matter; to management, it plainly wasn't. It seemed to us management didn't care about much. I had had enough of this no-care attitude and decided it was time to take action. I filed a complaint with the Facility Licensing and Investigations Section at the Department of Public Health, explaining the bed situation and mentioning other disturbing issues. I received a response the following week. They thanked me for my concern, said they would investigate, and that they would be in touch at the conclusion of their investigation.

I had given up all hopes of hearing from them when, on May 21, 2012, a representative called me at home. Our conversation lasted fifty-seven minutes! She was reading my concerns from my letter as we spoke, and I clarified each one. She asked if I had *new* concerns. I explained that the second shift (3:00 p.m. to 11:00 p.m.) was constantly understaffed, which I felt took away from my husband's care, as well as the other residents. This very pleasant state worker was at the facility handling their yearly review, and she said she would be there for a few more days and to let her know if I had anything else to report. The following morning she came to Ray's room before I had left to ask about his concerns, so I was able to meet her. The only one he addressed was his range of motion was being discontinued by the aides, who were told they could no longer perform range of motion on his body because they might hurt him. He was furious because this was something he desperately needed throughout the day, and he had been receiving it since he'd arrived. He had taken his concern to the nursing director, who told him it was now a "policy" and would no longer be a part of his daily routine. Ray needed that movement, not only for his muscles, but because of his blood pressure issues. This was just another example of the staff not knowing how to care for a quadriplegic. The state worker said she would definitely follow up on that. Ray and I liked her and we believed she would check into our concerns.

One day Ray heard, through the staff grapevine, that the staff believed that as long as his mattress was firm, it didn't need to "alternate air." This pissed him off, so he went to the staff doctor and his own doctor with his complaint. Finally, after almost a year, he received a new replacement mattress while his was finally repaired. In November 2011, his original mattress and motor were returned and seemed to be working as good as new.

Another change with this new management company was the influx of Alzheimer's and dementia residents. There was no locked unit in the facility, as there is in many other nursing homes. Ray's room was on the second floor, and that was where these residents were being placed, out of the view of visitors that entered the facility on the first floor. The ones that were still able to walk were left to wander around aimlessly, sometimes in their birthday suits, and they might urinate—or worse—right on the floor in view of everyone, even children. One resident hadn't been there twenty-four hours when she slapped another resident in the face. During her time at the facility, this particular resident urinated on the floor, walked naked in the hallway, and was found in the closet in someone else's room, naked from the waist up. She tried to take Ray's drainage bag from his wheelchair, but an aide stopped her before she succeeded. I saw her go behind the nurse's station when the nurse was elsewhere and walk away with one or two items. It was hard to monitor her constantly, because she wandered all over the second floor, and like a child could disappear in an instant. The final straw was when she started ripping Ray's giant-sized map of the United States off the wall. She already had the torn pieces in her hands when he entered his room and startled her. The facility reimbursed us the $100.00 and finally realized she needed to be in a secluded unit. Her family placed her in another facility.

Some residents in this state of mind are combative. Ray and I had seen nurses and aides get hit, kicked, punched, and bitten. More than once a resident would enter Ray's room and block the doorway so he couldn't get out. There was no talking to these residents, because they don't understand in the state of mind they're in. The only thing he could do was call me at work, via his voice-activated phone, and have me call the nurse's station and tell someone to get the resident out of the room.

Even when a person such as this leaves the facility, someone with similar issues is allowed in and the problems start all over again. Most management staff members leave around three to go to their happy homes and don't enter the facility until the next morning. The residents and staff members left behind are the ones that have to tolerate the behavior of these poor afflicted people. The ones in wheelchairs, and there are too many to count, are usually parked in the middle of the hallway, in front of the nurse's station, or in the residents' TV room, and Ray has a problem navigating his wheelchair around them. Most of the time he stays in his room to avoid becoming frustrated. They're also blocking doorways, entryways, and elevators. When Ray came to the facility, most of the residents were walking, but now there seems to be more and more in wheelchairs—and probably needlessly!

In the beginning of 2012, I didn't know if I could stand it anymore. Every night when I came in after work, there seemed to be a new issue. After not having hot water for a month, one evening the water was turned off at 8:00 p.m., which no one was aware of. There was minor construction being done in the facility and the workers were on-site, which might have contributed to the problem. Ray's aide attempted to fill a basin of water to clean him at bedtime and discovered an empty faucet. Luckily, he drinks bottled water which I purchase by the gallon, so the aide used that to wash him.

After it made a loud, rumbling noise for over a week, everyone could tell the ice machine was breaking down. When it finally stopped working, a cooler was filled with ice and placed at the nurse's station every day until a new, less expensive ice machine was purchased.

There had been talk of reducing staff hours, which would mean lay-offs for some, which would—again—reduce the residents' care. If someone asked me if I would recommend this facility for a loved one, my response would be, "Absolutely not!"

The only thing most of the upstairs staff enjoys is being in Ray's room. Everyone knows it's the place to hang out when you have a few minutes. There you can find out the latest gossip, get good advice on personal matters, have a cup of the best coffee in the house, and a quick treat to keep you going. You probably won't want Ray's leftover lunch or dinner however, because *no one* eats the foods that Ray likes, which includes anything and everything hot and spicy. Since the staff is of different ethnic backgrounds, he is willing to try whatever they bring him.

And if someone is in need of something, the first place they go is to Ray's room. They've asked for hair clips, peanut butter, milk, orange juice, a pen, Crystal Light, beef jerky, candy, mayonnaise, ketchup, bananas, the use of his phone, Tums, Advil, elastics, or just to step in for a few minutes during the hot summer months to take advantage of the air-conditioned environment. Even if he isn't in the room, they make themselves at home to complete their paperwork.

He's been told he has the most interesting door. Because it's metal, it's easy to display pictures of loved ones and other favorite people with magnets. However, you might find a flag, or a recent newspaper article about Ray marking the seventh anniversary of his accident, or Gina being a finalist in the bartender's contest in the Twin Cities, or even a special birthday wish. Different holidays are also recognized, with pictures of valentines, shamrocks, Easter bunnies, pumpkins, turkeys, and Santa Claus, even pictures of the CNA's new babies.

Even though there have been difficult times here and we've thought about moving to another facility, Ray likes that I am able to stay with him during the night and is afraid that wouldn't be allowed elsewhere. Plus, his personal doctor is affiliated with the facility, and his wheelchair was made and is serviced by the company that also services the wheelchairs here. So, for the time being he'll remain here and we'll try to make the best of it.

On March 2, 2012, Ray called to tell me that a certain staff member of the facility was gone, which to me was good news. A few months before, I had had a conversation with this person about an incident I was involved in. A resident, whose room was close to Ray's, could be heard throughout the entire wing, harassing and yelling obscenities at the aides because they didn't get him an ice cream or something else he may have demanded. His outburst upset our friends, who were in Ray's room visiting, so I went to the resident and told him to shut up. This particular staff member told that I would be banned from the facility if I didn't keep *my* mouth shut. I was also told that this was *his* house—meaning the resident—and that he could say whatever he wanted.

Although that staff member is gone, the resident is left to harass the aides, which disturbs other residents, especially his roommates. On one occasion, he had an argument with a roommate and threw his container of urine at him. The roommate fell and had to be taken to the hospital. When he returned, he was put in another room and the obnoxious resident remained. Of course, certain staff members have not been present when this resident has gotten unruly. I'm waiting for the day when justice prevails and this guy gets out of the vicinity of Ray's room!

One night I was awakened during the wee hours of the morning by Ray, because of the congestion lodged in his throat and his inability to cough it up. I went to his bedside and used the control to lower his head so he could lie flat, which sometimes helped. But, of course, this was not one of those times. I raised his head and went in the hallway to ask an aide for assistance. With her on one side and me on the other, we placed one hand under his arm and the other around his back. Next on the count of three, we rapidly thrust him forward so his face was almost touching his knees—but nothing happened. After a couple of tries, I dismissed the aide and decided a breathing treatment might help. The treatment lasted about eight minutes, which during the night when I'm extremely tired seems like an eternity. After the breathing treatment, I thought lowering his head again might loosen the phlegm. Not this time. I became angry and started to mutter nasty things, which I had a tendency to do when I'm tired. Things like: "Why does this always happen in the middle of the night? What did we ever do to deserve this life? I'm so tired and my sixty-seven-year-old body can't take much more." Then I feel bad because Ray always apologizes for putting me through this, when he's going through so much just trying to stay alive.

I lay down again and started to fall asleep, all the while listening to him coughing and hearing the loose junk in his throat that refused to budge. After I heard all I could stand, I got up again and lowered the head of the bed. Nothing! I went out in the hall and told the aide I needed her help again, and finally the congestion came up. After thanking her, I went back to bed, realizing that the time changed the next night—clocks went forward an hour. Oh, no. I could hardly afford to lose an hour's sleep!

Precisely at 7:00 the next morning, I was awakened by, "Sandra, wake up. It's time to get up." After the night I'd had, I could hardly open my eyes. Then I started muttering again about what a lousy life this was, how I was too old to be doing all this, how much my body hurt from lack of sleep, and about the hour of sleep I was going to lose that night. Sometimes I asked myself, "How can he still love me when I'm constantly complaining"

CHAPTER 6

||||||||||||||||||||||||||||||||||||||||||||||||||||||||||||||||||||||||||||||||||||||||||||||||||

The Fundraiser

I welcome change as a great adventure.
Jonathan Lockwood Huie

Ray's visitors were his only contact to the outside world for the first eight months after his accident. I updated my family, our close friends, and his cousin Lois by e-mail daily.

Ray's elderly Aunt Ruth from New Jersey came several times on the bus from her home to the casino. I, or someone from my family, would pick her up at the casino and bring her to visit with Ray. Just before the bus left for the return trip, we'd get her back to the casino. She has visited him at each facility.

My parents visited weekly until their illnesses, and usually spent an hour or two talking about current events, baseball, and family members. My brothers came when they could. My sister usually brought something for him to eat, and her fiancée came once a week.

Before the fund-raiser, we knew we had to have a vehicle that could transport Ray. When I purchased my Uplander on February 1, 2005, I bought it with the intention of accessorizing it to accommodate Ray's needs. Prior to that, my parents and my friends

Carol and Stan had accompanied me to a dealership where they sell and accessorize vehicles for the handicapped. I was shown what it would entail to enhance a vehicle as well as the cost of a used vehicle, which was quite hefty. When I went back there in August with my new vehicle, the salesman took one look at it and told me it could not be accessorized to meet Ray's needs. Oh, no! Would I have to trade it in and purchase a handicapped van?

I thought perhaps a familiar area dealership could be of help, so I made an appointment. I explained the situation and the salesmen told me that they could probably purchase a vehicle at a car auction, accessorize it, give me $17,000 for mine, and only charge me an additional $15,000. I broke down right in front of them because I couldn't believe my brand new vehicle was worth $20,000 less than what I had paid for it just six months earlier. Plus, I didn't want to deplete my savings, which were quickly dwindling on things I needed *after* I had gone through the spend down. Why hadn't someone told us to keep some of our money "for a rainy day," because we were certainly having a lot of them. It took me several minutes to compose myself, and then I told them I'd think it over, even though I knew damn well I was never going back to accept that offer.

I heard of another place that sold used vans, and my daughter and Samanthia accompanied me when I went to see what they had to offer. I was immediately disappointed and we returned home. Now I didn't know what to do now. I decided to call the specialty dealership and ask them if they could bring a vehicle to the nursing home for Ray to see, and then we could both find out exactly what was entailed in getting him in and out. The salesman was kind enough to bring one down, but Ray could not get into it because it was too small. The salesman and I checked the Internet together and found one that we thought would work. I would have to make a $1,000 deposit, since the vehicle had to be transported from another state. At the same time my brother Dick checked out an old ambulance that was selling for $3,500. He thought it was worth looking at, but when I saw it I knew it wasn't going to work for us. That was our last experience with vans, because shortly after that Ray was sick a few times and I had to keep canceling my appointments with the salesman.

The first time Ray was able to go out in public was eight months after his accident, on May 27, 2005. He went to our great-niece Madison's first birthday, which was being held at my parents' home. Our newspaper reporter and photographer had told us they wanted to capture his first outing in words and pictures, since it would be an important event in our lives. However, my family was strongly opposed to this. My father said he didn't want "them" there, and my brother told me that this day "is not about Ray, it's all about Madison." I called the reporter with this news that had broken my heart, and then I cried all afternoon because I felt that my family had let me down. I had thought they would be happy for me, because this was the first time I was able to be out with my husband in over eight months. We were both so upset and talked about not going, but because we loved Madison, we knew being there was the right thing to do. One of the girls from the recreation department had possession of the handicapped van that the facility occasionally used, and she transported us. He did very well, enjoying being out in the fresh air and away from the busy nursing home. He immediately started looking forward to his next outing. Thank goodness the warm weather had arrived, because he had been cooped up all during the long cold winter.

The next time we went out happened to be for a barbecue with my family. They set up a portable ramp so Ray was able to go up on the deck. An ambulance transported us for our two-and-a-half-hour visit, and Ray was anxious to return to the nursing home when the ambulance came to pick us up.

On July 3 we went to a birthday celebration for our good friend Joe, and our transportation once again was an ambulance, which was paid for by senior resources through the Recreation Department at the nursing home. It was a wonderful day. Ray totally enjoyed himself, thanks to our friends, who went out of their way to make sure everything was perfect. However, when the time approached for the return to the nursing home, he was eager to go. After all, that was his comfort zone, the place he had called home for the last six months.

In August, we were invited to our friend Judy's sixtieth birthday celebration. A driver from a private company picked us up at 5:00 p.m. and we returned at 9:00 p.m. We had a great time, and Ray became more relaxed each time he went out.

A very welcome visitor was one of Ray's good friends and former coworker from California. Jim, along with his wife and son. They drove from their second home in Pennsylvania in August 2005 and spent the night at our condo. Ray reminisced with Jim while his wife, Elaine, took me to dinner. They visited again in June 2011. Paul was another longtime friend from California. He and his wife Judy visited in April 2010 and again in April 2011 on their way to their hometown of Boston.

Gina came home in September 2005 for Ray's birthday celebration, which was his first since the accident. I had planned a big event. I was always so excited when she came home, and this time it was extra special because she genuinely enjoyed being with Ray. The first time this had been apparent was the year before at Thanksgiving, when she had kissed him good-bye. The feeling in my heart at that moment was something I hadn't experienced before. Another wonderful memory was the first time she called to wish him a Happy Father's Day. She and Ray hadn't always gotten along, which had been stressful to me at times, but they both seemed to forget all that after Ray's accident. When I mentioned to Ray how happy I was that it finally felt that we were a family, his reaction was, "Then it was meant to be." Several years later, when Gina and I were out to dinner on one of her visits home, I mentioned this conversation to her and tears glistened in her eyes. She said that Ray had changed. Her opinion was that he had been angry a lot before the accident, but now he was more mellow and easier to talk to, which seemed strange, considering what he'd been through.

September 10, 2005, was his sixty-second birthday and the first time he would enter our home since the accident 364 days ago. I sent invitations that read:

**THIS IS AN INVITATION FOR A VERY
SPECIAL BIRTHDAY PARTY
FOR A VERY REMARKABLE MAN**

<u>RAY HOCKING</u>

**Please come to an impromptu gathering
of friends and family at an open
house on Saturday, September 10,
beginning at 1pm and lasting
throughout the afternoon.**

**Look for the balloons>>>>>>>>>>>>>>>>>>>>>>>
>>>THAT'S THE CLUBHOUSE!!!!!!!**

Again, he was transported by a private company. It would be the first time he would use the fifty-foot ramp my brother Dick had built. After a little hesitation and checking out the ramp he'd never seen before, he drove his brand new battery-powered wheelchair up that wooden highway like a pro. He made it through the sliding door to the dining room while the crowd cheered and pictures were taken. He drove through the dining room, through the kitchen, and into the living room, where he checked out his large salt-water fish tank. While he was in the kitchen, he never took a second look at the place where he had fallen a year ago. Finally, he was ready to go to his birthday party, which was being held at our condo association's clubhouse. There was another long, winding uphill ramp to climb, but he finally made it. He was amazed at the many balloons and the tables laden with food, gifts, and pictures. Approximately one hundred of our family and friends came to celebrate during the course of the afternoon. Among them were two of Ray's longtime lineman friends, Jeff and Joe, who'd flown in from California to surprise him. Ray was ecstatic to see them. They had brought a collage of photographs from their work days together, some showing Ray 120 feet in the air working on 230,000-volt lines. They reminisced about the entertainment they had provided whenever they indulged in a cocktail or two. They also had a few words to say about their longtime friend, Ray.

"He hasn't lost his sense of humor," Joe said. "His spirit is still the Ray Hocking spirit that I always knew."

"All these months I've been talking to him on the phone," Jeff said, "and not once has there been a word out of his mouth like *poor me*. He's a good man."

I'm so grateful to the many people that helped make this first birthday celebration a great success. It made one special man very happy!

Ray's cousin Lois and her husband Bill stopped by on a road trip from Pennsylvania to Vermont one weekend in October 2005. We watched the video of Ray's birthday celebration together, because they had been unable to attend. When Lois left on Monday, I'm sure her mind was at ease knowing that Ray was still in good spirits in spite of his injury.

His most loyal visitors, Judy and Joe, come every Friday night. The amazing thing is that they thoroughly enjoy his company as much as he enjoys theirs, and he looks forward to their visits each and every week. They arrive around eight, and it has become a tradition for Joe to feed Ray dinner. Since Joe doesn't eat a lot of the different foods that Ray does, he's gotten an education in many dishes he's never heard of before, such as tofu, quinoa, couscous, squid, sausage, and peppers, and Italian food featuring garlic and spices. Each week we do a little trivia game, and they're amazed at Ray's knowledge of history, geography and current events. They have become acquainted with the staff and some of the residents, and we laugh when someone says that Joe would make a good public relations director for the nursing home. I don't know how I would have gotten through this without their friendship and support. They always call to see if Ray wants anything special, and sometimes they bring a surprise when they come. The first Christmas they brought a bottle of my favorite perfume, accompanied by a beautiful card—and the look on Ray's face was priceless when I realized it was my Christmas present from him. They did the same on Valentine's Day. This became a tradition for each holiday.

The newly elected mayor of our town was a childhood friend from my old neighborhood. I e-mailed him to see if he could come and meet Ray. Instead of answering my e-mail, he immediately called my cell phone and arranged a date for him to visit us. He and Ray hit it off instantly, and he told Ray he needed to get out of the nursing home "and we're going to get you a van." He decided to launch a fund-raiser, and a mutual friend, Greg, agreed to be cochairman. We had become friendly with Greg and his family when his father was a resident.

Every time Gina called me, she made a point of asking about Ray. When she found out about the fund-raiser, she decided that she would like to host a fund-raiser in her hometown. I had gotten to know many of her friends—many of whom played in bands—from my visits to Minneapolis, and they were well aware of Ray's situation. I was completely overwhelmed by such an awesome gesture, and when I told Ray, he was equally overwhelmed. They decided to do the fund-raiser on Saturday, June 3.

Ray's pictures appeared in the newspaper on Sunday, April 10, 2006, with an article titled "Community Rallies to Aid Paralyzed Man." The article stated that "the Hockings will visit their prospective van at 10:00 a.m. today at a dealership in town with the mayor and dealership owner in attendance."

A reporter and cameraman from our local news channel was there, as well as a reporter and photographer from the area newspapers. We met the custodian of the bank account that had been set up to receive donations.

That evening Ray had his thirty seconds of fame on TV, as the news program ran the story of the van that had been donated to launch the campaign to raise $25,000. Ray told how the van would help him achieve his independence by enabling him to get out more.

The next day, both local papers had articles and pictures, explaining the fund-raiser and how it got started with the mayor's visit to Ray in March.

My brother came to the nursing home during the first week in May with fire in his eyes. He had been researching handicapped vans, our prospective van in particular, and told us that the van didn't cost anywhere near $25,000. It cost under $10,000! He was furious because he thought a paralyzed man was being taken advantage of to make money for a car dealer. He said he was still researching and would have all the information available to me soon. Two days later he called to say that he was going to the dealership that afternoon. He would inform them of his findings and demand that they rectify the situation, or he would write his own article in the newspaper!

After speaking to the garage owner my brother had a change of heart, and admitted that he should have talked to him before he did his research. He could have saved himself a lot of aggravation. However, the owner said he understood Dick's purpose and respected him for being as aggressive as he was. He told Dick he would keep him abreast of any new information.

I relayed this news to Ray and could hear the relief in his voice. Not because he didn't believe in everyone and what was being done to help us, but because now my brother could inform my family. Up until then there had been little conversation about the fund-raiser, and he'd be able to tell them what a wonderful thing it is.

I received a call from the custodian of the bank account. He gave me the specifics on the van and asked me to call my insurance company and get a quote for the first year, because this was to be included in the cost. That was a wonderful unexpected surprise. We had certainly teamed up with a great bunch of people. He also told me that the expected delivery date of the van was May 24 or 25. How exciting for us!

During this time I heard from a classmate of mine who lived in Tucson, Arizona. When she heard about the fund-raiser, she e-mailed several of our classmates, told them of my situation, and asked for their help. This is the e-mail she sent:

April 14, 2006
Dear Classmate:
The enclosed article from the newspaper concerns our classmate Sandy Occhionero's husband, Ray Hocking. I hope after you read the article you will make a donation to

the "Wheels for Ray Hocking" fund-raiser. Any amount will help. The mayor is doing his best to assist them. Thank you for your consideration ... imagine if you were in their place. I know Sandy and Ray appreciate any help you may provide, whether it's a donation or prayers.

Thank you, and I hope to see you at the 45th reunion in 2007...

I will always be grateful to Maureen, and I owe her a huge thank you because many classmates contributed. I'm very thankful to those classmates too, because after all these years, it was wonderful to know they were still the same great "kids" I'd known in school.

My cousin Ora and her husband Roger presented us with a card containing money collected from several of their immediate family members. Roger had additional funds to offer us from a local union.

Finally on May 24, 2006, we were picked up at the nursing home and taken to a luncheon where we were the guests of honor, along with the participants of the fund-raiser. It was a touching moment when the mayor told the crowd what an inspiration Ray had been—and still was—to so many people. I was presented with the keys to the van. I wanted to thank everyone, but I was too overwhelmed to speak.

Our next stop was the dealership, which took about an hour and a half while they registered and insured the van, and then filled it with gas. When it was time to leave, I sat behind the wheel for the first time while Ray was directed onto the lift. On the way back to the nursing home, we stopped for some take-out. Finally, it was time for us to unload at the nursing home, and I have to say, our first time was perfect. That gave us a lot of confidence. We had done did it! We had overcome the first big hurdle with the help of some generous people.

The next time I saw Gina was when I went to Minneapolis to attend the benefit for Ray, which took place on June 3, 2006. Again I brought my friend Samanthia with me. She and I stayed at a bed and breakfast close to Gina's house. There were several places for us to go that weekend. We went to an art exhibit in the park, and Gina and the other two Shim Sham Shufflers danced during the band's intermission. They also danced at the benefit that evening, and I learned that Gina had made all the costumes. What a talented lady! The benefit was very successful, and since we already had the van, this money would be used for therapy and equipment that was not covered by insurance. After I returned home, I sent a note of thanks:

When Ray and I first heard that you wanted to help with a fund-raiser of your own, it actually brought tears to our eyes. It's the most thoughtful and generous thing that any daughter could possibly do and we are truly grateful, and very lucky that we have you as "our" daughter. You're so smart and talented and loving and beautiful, and I'm so proud of the woman you've become and I love you very much!

WE THANK YOU FROM THE BOTTOM OF OUR HEARTS

I got a list of the contributors from the custodian of the bank account because we wanted to thank each and every one of them for their generosity. The amount of the individual contributions was never revealed. It was not important. That list included friends, a few coworkers, and others that I did not recognize but whom I assumed followed our story. There was even a donation from the local high school. I also received cards in the mail from two woman I had never met. Each had a $1,000 check enclosed with a note stating that they, too, had ailing husbands they cared for and they wanted to help us. This horrible accident that had changed our lives in a split second had taught me that people do care about others and put their own troubles aside to offer help when it's needed, even to those they don't know.

Our thank you notes went out on June 17, 2006.

THANK YOU FROM THE BOTTOM OF OUR HEARTS

Ray and I are extremely grateful for your generosity and would like to thank you for helping us achieve our dream of having our own handicapped vehicle. It's amazing how many people have been following our story and have helped us through the most difficult time of our lives. You can never imagine, in your wildest dreams, how your happy, perfect life can change in a split second. Thanks to you, and so many other wonderful people, we can once again experience the freedom that we thought was lost forever!

We will always remember our first outing after the fund-raiser because it was the first time we were alone with the van. We had thought it was going to be fun and easy, but no way. First the hydraulic lift did not work properly. It would fold out but would not lower. I pressed the lever several times and still it would not move. I called the nurse's station and one of the aides offered her assistant. The first time she tried, she was successful! Ray had to maneuver himself in the proper position so I could lock him in. When I got down on the floor, I could not remember where to place the hooks on his chair. It was so hot, I thought I was going to pass out. Forty-five minutes later, after several tries and some sputtering, I finally got him situated and we drove away.

We arrived at our friend's house, and I was not about to go through the hassle of getting him out of the van and get all upset again, so I let our friends take over. They didn't seem to have as much of a problem as I did, so we were able to finally enjoy the day.

While I was at my daughter's benefit in Minneapolis, Ray took another ride in the van with some friends, who also had a problem with the lift. However, his outing was great. It did have to be transferred indoors because of rain, while my weather in Minneapolis was sunny and in the eighties. I was so glad he got to go out while I was away, because I knew how lonely he got without me.

Shortly after my return from Minneapolis, Ray had a doctor's appointment. I managed to get him in the van with some assistance from someone in the Recreation Department. Somehow Ray was able to exit the van and see the doctor, but when the time came to get him back in the van, I got very nervous. He had to recline his chair so far back to get in the van, I feared he was going to tip over. I just couldn't do it! I started to hyperventilate; I was so certain he would fall off the lift. A friend from the doctor's office and some construction workers who were working close by managed to get him safely in the van. After I had calmed down and slid in the driver's seat, I was finally ready for the ride back to the nursing home. I called ahead to make sure someone was available to help get him out of the van for the day's last exit!

The next time we went out in the van, it seemed to take forever. I was nervous again because of the sensation that the lift will not hold him, along with his having to recline his chair so far down. It took so long that by the time we got halfway to our destination, which was for a Fourth of July family picnic, we were both so nervous, we decided to turn around and go back where we felt safe. As I was lowering the lift, I realized that the two small back wheels on the chair were still in the vehicle while the rest of the chair—with him in it—was being lowered. Of course I panicked, because it looked like he was going to fall face first onto the pavement. Luckily, when I screamed, someone came out of the nursing home and knew exactly what to do to help get him out. By this time I was hyperventilating again. That was the last time I took him in the van!

On September 10, 2006, for Ray's sixty-third birthday, we had a celebration at a park by the water on a beautiful sunny day with many friends and relatives in attendance. This invitation read:

SECOND ANNUAL BIRTHDAY CELEBRATION
For
RAY HOCKING

I would like to extend an invitation for you to join me in celebrating an event that is very important to me. My husband, Ray Hocking, is having a birthday on Sept 10 and I have reserved the LAKESIDE PAVILLION. Last year's birthday celebration was very special. It was the first time he was inside our home since his accident the year before. Many friends and family members helped to celebrate this momentous event. He was especially happy to see his two longtime friends who came all the way from California to personally wish him a "Happy Birthday."

He was able to be transported in his own van, driven by John, who had become his primary driver. John was the gentleman I met in the hospital waiting room when I took my niece for a walk so her mother and father could visit with Ray. At the time, John was in a wheelchair, having just had an operation on his foot. I introduced myself and told him about Ray. After that initial meeting, he visited Ray frequently until he left the hospital. We didn't hear from John until Ray was settled in at the nursing home. After we got the van, John agreed to be Ray's driver. He took him to church every Sunday, drove him to his birthday celebrations, took him to appointments, drove him home to spend time with me on my days off, and even took the van for maintenance whenever necessary. It was great, because he was available whenever Ray needed or wanted to leave the facility. John got married, however, and became busy doing things with his wife. Although we were happy for John, this was unfortunate for us, because now we didn't have a driver readily available.

Having missed the first birthday celebration, Ray's cousin Lois was able to attend the second one, which made him very happy. Again friends from his work and mine were there, as well as family members, and some people even came from the nursing home. We cooked hamburgers on the grill and a good time was had by all. That was the last of the large birthday celebrations. After that he preferred small family gatherings. Subsequent ones were held at the facility with only family in attendance. However, in 2011 we celebrated his birthday at our home, because he hadn't been out in quite some time while the van had been being serviced.

Lois's daughter Dawn and her new husband David paid Ray a visit late in September 2006. Dave was attending a business conference at the casino, and Dawn thought it would be a great opportunity to spend the day with Ray. It happened to be my day off, so I was able to spend the time with them also. It was great seeing her and meeting Dave, whom Ray liked immediately. We could both see how happy they were with each other.

My childhood friend Carol and her husband Stan come occasionally with a home-cooked meal, and the four of us would get to enjoy one of her excellent creations. This was always a treat for us, because we hardly ever get to eat home cooking. Our meals consisted of take-out, which was something we never had in our "other life." After the first five years we thought, *enough* with the take-out. I began cooking on my days off, and we were able to enjoy the foods we loved once again.

As the years go on, the visitors change. The ones that were constants in the beginning have grown distant. Sometimes days go by without a familiar face, and the days are long and lonely when there's no one to talk to. At times I've felt that Ray's been forgotten by many people who came to see him in the beginning, people whose visits got less frequent as time went on. I feel so bad when he mentions that a certain person hasn't been around for a while. We realize people are busy with their own lives, but they have no idea of what it's like to be in a nursing home twenty-four hours a day, seven days a week, with no one to talk to except the staff, and that's only if they have free time. That's why it's so important to see a familiar face and be able to have a healthy conversation. Once we got the van, it was different, because he could escape those walls for a while. We had hoped more people would volunteer to drive the van and learn the intricacies of the lift and the procedure of securing the wheelchair, but unfortunately, only a few have offered. It's disappointing, because if he had more drivers, he would be able to get out more.

My Aunt Alice had a special birthday celebration in April 2008 when she turned 100. She was a resident of another nursing home, and Ray was present for that milestone.

In July 2009, my Aunt Rainey, Uncle Joe, and cousin Tim visited from Arizona and spent a few hours with Ray. Visiting them in May 2004 had been the last vacation we had together before the accident. They spent the afternoon with us at the nursing home, and we watched an interesting DVD of my uncle being interviewed on the History Channel, speaking of his experience in the Flying Tigers during World War II.

In August 2009, my nephew Richard, who lived in California, flew to a neighboring state for his job. He took a few extra days to visit my parents when my father became ill. Ray was excited because he thought Richard would visit him too, and was disappointed when he didn't have the time. Since Ray hadn't had the opportunity to thank Richard for coming all that way to see him when he first got hurt and was in CCU, he thought he would finally have the opportunity.

After a few times out in our new van, we realized it was too much of a hassle for Ray to get in and out, because he had to recline the wheelchair in an almost lying down position. We found out about a foundation that offered grants to qualified handicapped persons so they could add height to their vans. I wrote to them and explained our situation.

My husband is a quadriplegic, as a result of a fall in our kitchen on 9/11/04. He broke his neck at level C4/C5 and has no movement in his arms and legs. He was a power lineman for 38 years and just turned 61 years old on 9/10/04. He is presently on Title 19. We had to liquidate all our assets, which were very impressive, and I became his Power of Attorney. Needless to say, when it came time to acquire a handicap accessible van, our funds were depleted. The mayor of our town came to visit us at the "skilled" nursing facility where my husband resides and decided to host a fund-raiser which would enable us to have a van so he could once again see the outside world. The fund-raiser was successful and we were presented with a 2000 Ford Econoline van with a lift. However, he has to recline his chair to practically a vertical position to enter the van so we have not been able to utilize this generous gift very often. Another paralyzed person told us about your foundation and that you may be able to help us with a grant. We need to heighten the van and improve the lift. We got a verbal estimate for both, with a promise of a written one. His doctor also signed a statement explaining his quadriplegia, which we knew you would need.

After a short time I received a call with the good news that Ray was indeed qualified. With the enhancement of the van, which was of no cost to us, Ray was able to enter and exit without a problem. Yes, we were very happy with the finished product!

He was able to join my family at the assisted living facility where my parents were living for Thanksgiving and Christmas 2010, with my brother's assistance driving the van. They were happy events, especially Christmas, because my daughter made a surprise visit all the way from Minnesota!

My parents weren't able to be with us in 2011 for the holidays. My mother was suffering from the onset of Alzheimer's and my father had several health issues, so I decided to have my brothers and sister over to my home for Thanksgiving. My brother went to pick up Ray, and the lift on the van wouldn't lower. After a few attempts, Dick knew it was futile. Even if it did work after that, Ray would not go for the simple fact that it might malfunction again when it was time for him to return to the nursing home. Needless to say, I was very disappointed. When Christmastime came and we wanted to be together again, we all agreed to gather at the nursing home on Christmas Eve, where we knew Ray could join us.

After having the lift repaired, we thought March 17, 2012, would be a good time to get together, and Ray suggested cooking on the grill. The weather was favorable but Ray wasn't able to join us because the lift let us down once again. Another disappointment. Sometimes it seems if we didn't have bad luck, we wouldn't have any luck at all!

The van was taken to a company that specialized in handicapped vehicles. The lift was repaired and the van was cleaned and detailed, which would enable Ray to make it to the next gathering. In June 2012, three nieces were in town, so I thought it would be great to have the family together. Ray was not able to join us *once again* because it was pouring rain and he was concerned about the wheelchair.

The fifty-foot ramp at my house has no overhang and Ray did not want to risk the chair getting wet and possibly malfunctioning. He decided to stay at the nursing home and out of the rain. It was great to see my brother Mike's children, Michael, Jenny and Danny, as well as his wife Jody, and two of my brother Dick's children, Mark and Dina, as well as his granddaughter Madison. My sister Debby's fiancée, Bob, was also in attendance. We all had a great time. Of course our parents were unable to be with us, but that wasn't going to change. We had learned to accept it.

There are a few frequent visitors that Ray sees three or four times a month, and a few retired power company coworkers who come a couple times a year.

His niece Abby, his nephew Brendan, and his sister-in-law Karen come from New Jersey to visit whenever their work schedules allow, and they stay at our condo. They love Ray and Abby and Brendan look to him as a father figure, since their father—Ray's brother—passed away. Ray couldn't love them more if they were his own children. Ray only spoke to his brother, Hugh, by phone after Ray got injured. Hugh was suffering with cancer and passed away shortly after Ray's accident. Unfortunately, they hadn't see each other for several years.

His relatives keep in constant touch by telephone because they all live in other states, as do his longtime friends in California. He enjoys each and every call, because they keep him connected to the outside world. And with his voice-activated phone, which he whistles on and off, he can make phone calls himself.

Of course, there are visits from people who have not forgotten about him after all these years. Two frequent visitors are brothers, Chris and Greg. They visit a couple times every month, and Ray always has a story to tell them about his adventures restoring power, or the crazy stunts he pulled with his fellow linemen, or the amazing sights he'd witnessed during his travels around the country. He loves to make people laugh whenever he has an audience. He's been told by a few people that he could be a stand-up comedian. Pardon the pun. One crazy story we've heard is when he was younger and living in California, he went out one night and had a few drinks. At the time, he had a new Porsche and didn't feel he should drive it home. He called for a taxi and upon its arrival, realized he didn't want to leave his Porsche either, so he asked the cab driver if he would like to drive it. Of course he said he would, so Ray drove the cab home and the taxi driver followed in the Porsche!

Another regular visitor is Jerry, who comes for a few hours every Saturday. We met Jerry and his wife Debbie when Debbie's father was a resident of the facility. After he passed away, we remained friends and they were very helpful with the fund-raiser.

Willy is also a frequent visitor and good friend. Ray and I met Willy when his father was a resident, and he continues to come to the facility to see Ray and a few others he met during his father's convalescence. He's become one of Ray's transporters and helps with the van whenever it needs maintenance. He was very persistent in urging me to tell my story.

My brother Dick was the primary driver for a few years and continues to transport Ray when needed. He has taken him to doctor and dentist appointments, but most especially to our home when we gather with family and friends on special occasions.

We've also been able to depend on Carol, whom we met while she was working at the nursing home. Her son also suffers from quadriplegia, so she knows the procedure with the lift. Whenever she's available, she gracefully volunteers.

I know I will never feel confident taking Ray in the van. I always have the notion that the lift won't hold him and he'll fall again. Since I almost let that happen once, I'll be forever grateful to these wonderful people, all of whom Ray feels comfortable with, who volunteer their time so he can escape that busy place for a few hours!

CHAPTER 7

Private Moments

***What lies behind us and what lies before us
are tiny matters compared to what lies
within us. Ralph Waldo Emerson***

When Ray was first in the hospital and was transferred to a private room after two weeks in CCU, I brought the basket of cards, letters, mass cards, and e-mails. Standing at his bedside, I began reading them to him. Many times I had to stop and dry my eyes before I could proceed to the next. So many were affected by our situation, which was evident by the well wishes that had already totaled two hundred! He was overwhelmed, having no idea what had occurred while he was in CCU.

He told me the one thing he did remember was having an out-of-body experience. He looked down and could see doctors and nurses working on his body. He knew he was going to survive because during this "adventure," he was told it was not his time and to go back.

One night, during the wee hours, while at the rehabilitation hospital, he got really sick with congestion and was having a hard time breathing. The nurse knew she had to suction the mucus out of his lungs, which wasn't an easy task now that he no longer had the trache button in his neck. They had to insert tubes in his nose that would reach down his throat and into his lungs. I could not watch, so I stepped out into the hallway with tears running down my cheeks. When it was over, I held him and we both cried. It was the first time he talked about dying. He told me that if he didn't pull through, I was to have his body cremated and then have his ashes buried with me.

After our first few weeks at the nursing home, we had several conversations about the absence of visitors, which had been so much in our lives at the out-of-town hospitals. I told him more than once we were the forgotten ones. He said that he'd known it would be like that once the "novelty" wore off. I said, "It's you and me against the world." I told him how sad it made me that some people didn't come to visit anymore, and he told me what he always says whenever I get upset about anything: **don't try to change something you can't**. He told me the one thing he missed more than anything was having someone to talk to. I felt bad, because I could leave for eight hours a day, but he had to stay and endure the boredom. Sometimes days would go by without seeing a familiar face or having a friendly conversation.

One evening in the privacy of our room, Ray admitted that in the beginning, before we understood the severity of his paralysis, he thought that perhaps the break in his neck might not be permanent. He thought because he was in good health, exercised, always watched what he ate, never smoked, never did drugs, that he could overcome this. However, when he finally realized that he would be permanently paralyzed, his attitude was amazing. As he stated, things could have been worse. He was lucky he was sixty-one years old and not twenty-one!

The first time we started making plans to go home, we had a few meetings with social workers. They told us we had to apply for a PCA (patient care attendant) waiver, which would allow us to have a number of paid hours agreed on by the state for home care. It was decided to allow us fifty-six hours, which weren't nearly enough. We knew Ray would need twenty-four hours of home care daily, seven days a week. That left us with about 110 hours that we would have to supplement. We were given a release date of February 14, 2006. We were excited and eager to leave, but we had to hire the health care workers we needed. I approached about five CNAs (certified nursing assistants) that had cared for Ray and had expressed an interest in taking care of him at home. However, weeks went by and not one of them responded. Time was marching on, and I felt like we weren't accomplishing anything. At a meeting, the social workers asked us what kind of a bed and Hoyer Lift we wanted. It seemed that everything was being left up to us, and we were wondering what the heck we had social workers for! One night while relaxing in the room, we started expressing our feelings to each other. We realized that with all we were expected to do, we were getting stressed, and decided the time was not right to leave. It would be easier to stay put for the time being.

We were so upset with the health care system and the obstacles we were always up against, that I wrote an article that appeared in our newspaper on March 5, 2006.

Trapped by Rules, a Difficult Life Gets Even Harder

My husband, Ray, had a terrible accident on Sept.11, 2004, one day after his 61st birthday and he has been living in a nursing home for the last 13 months. He fell in the kitchen of our home and broke his neck, which resulted in his becoming paralyzed below the chest. He will never walk or use his arms again without a miracle. Before his accident, he was a lineman for nearly 40 years.

Ray is currently on Title 19 (Medicaid). Every day we become frustrated and more aware that "the system" needs to be completely revised.

In order to become eligible for Medicaid, Connecticut required us to "spend down" our assets. Prior to this, we had enough money for a van and for a physical therapist, neither of which are included under the Medicaid insurance. Therapy is very important to a paralyzed person, but Title 19 puts my husband in the category of "custodial care," because, with his injury, he's not expected to improve. If the staff have time they put a hot pack on his shoulder and massage it. Ray has continual shoulder pain, a common complaint with a spinal cord injury. He needs an adjustment to his wheelchair to ease the pain. The paperwork was submitted to Medicaid 12 weeks ago because funds need to be approved before an adjustment can be made.

Meanwhile, he suffers every day.

I've been trying to find help to purchase a handicap vehicle. I bought a 2005 Chevrolet Uplander a year ago for $39,000, as part of our "spend down," because I thought it could be accommodated for his handicap. Six months after I bought it, I decided to trade it for one that he could utilize. Sadly, I was told that it was only worth $17,000. This is doubly frustrating, because the vehicle he needs cost $40,000. With the purchase of a van, I could take him to our home, where he's only been once since his accident.

Ray never gets to see the outside world anymore. The facility does not own a van, and since we cannot afford one, he remains inside. An ambulance service will only transport for medical emergencies and if he has to go to the dentist or has a doctor's appointment. They will not take Medicaid wheelchair patients without a 48-hour notice. The only other transportation is a private transport company, which we have used, but on the weekends it costs more because a driver is not readily available. Without transportation, we spent this past Christmas Eve at the nursing home, instead of home with the family. Last year's Christmas Eve was spent in a tiny room at the rehabilitation hospital.

Ray was finally going to come home on Valentine's Day, but with his many admittances to the hospital because of urinary tract infections, we decided that now is not a good time, so he will continue to live at the nursing home for a while longer. He's been in the hospital three times since New Year's Day. Also, trying to obtain home care is difficult. We need skilled, licensed Certified Nursing Assistants. Medicaid will fund 58 hours a week ... which leaves 110 hours unpaid that we are responsible for.

The sad thing is that my husband does not belong in a convalescent home that is not equipped to deal with a quadriplegic. Ray should be in a place with professionals who are trained to treat him and those with similar injuries.

I just wish there were a little extra help out there for people in our situation who are forced to give up assets and any semblance of normalcy because of a situation that, without warning, changed our lives forever.

In August 2006, after being released from the hospital for pneumonia, a urinary tract infection and suprapubic catheter operation, Ray told me that he was lying awake during the night and thinking he was going to die ... and wishing he would! I asked him why he would think that after all this time. His reply was that he was worried about me and what he's putting me through, and that he's afraid it's getting too much for me. If he dies, it would make my life easier. He said that when he does die, to keep his ashes close to me and don't be too sad. I bent down to cradle his head in my arms and we both cried. He hadn't had many moments like that, but this last hospitalization was one of the worst he'd had to endure. He had been in a room where he couldn't see out the door, and since he's claustrophobic it was tough for him to be alone for several hours. He would ask for a Xanax just to get him through the hours until I arrived. I cried every time I left him. Sometimes I felt so bad and couldn't even control the tears until I got to my car.

A few months later we thought perhaps the time was right to plan our "great escape." Again we met with the social workers and the procedure was repeated. This time the state approved sixty-six hours of home health care, which left us with about one hundred and two hours we would have to pay for. I was given a list of licensed PCAs, most of whom resided outside our immediate area. Again we thought it was not the right time. There was so much to do just to get him home, and then there would be the added pressure of shopping for supplies, picking up medications and arranging meals, all of which was taken care of while he resided at the nursing home. And we knew what would happen if a scheduled aide couldn't come for some reason. His care would be left up to me, and there were some things I couldn't or wouldn't do.

Again we decided that the time wasn't right and that he would be a resident of this place indefinitely. There would be no more plans of leaving, which was a discouraging realization. Sometimes it seemed unbearable. We both understood at that time that there were only a handful of people working at the facility that we could trust. Some of the nurses and aides truly cared and were very compassionate, while others were there just for the paycheck or because there was nothing else they could do. We knew details about many of the staff members' private lives, since Ray's room was the place to go if you needed or wanted to know anything. We listened as the many single mothers complained about child care or the married ones talked about their unfaithful spouses.

For Ray and me, most of our private moments take place in this room. In the morning, our routine is consistent, even regimental. It's up at 7:00 with Ray calling out to me, "Sandra, it's time to get up." My reply is usually, "Oh, no. I wish I had one more hour." I struggle to get out of my bed and over to his, take off his Venodynes, and then raise his head in the bed and lower his legs. Next I set up his breathing treatment and make that delicious strong coffee that we've come to love. I always make extra because I never know who might stop in when they smell it brewing. We have breakfast together before I perform range-of-motion exercises. He's usually pretty stiff in the morning, and the motion loosens up his muscles. Sometimes it's a struggle for me. His arms and legs are very heavy—and I am getting older and weaker! But it makes him feel good, so I'll keep on struggling as long as I can.

The nurse takes his blood pressure every morning and brings in his pills. He washes them down with two containers of milk. After I wash his face and brush his teeth, it's time to decide what shirt he will wear, long sleeves or short. If it's a massage day, I write a check for $75, which I do three times a week! I wash the coffee cups, replenish his juice with enough to last him until I get back, and I put his watch on his wrist. We've joked about that because it's a self-winding rolex watch, and I have to shake it every morning and night because his arms don't move.

When I return from work, the first thing I do is empty my suitcase of the clean clothes I've brought him and refill it with the ones he wore that day, and then I change out of my work clothes. As I do this, we both review our days since we last spoke. We always have a snack, which might consist of potato chips, ice cream, cheese and crackers, candy.... Yes, it's our crazy time when we eat anything we feel like eating. It might not always be healthy and nutritious, but considering where we are, sometimes we just *need* to eat crazy. Just before 11:00, I brush and floss his teeth. The night crew gets him into the position he desires, and it's lights out until 2:00 a.m., when he's repositioned.

In early 2009, we had a few frustrating days. The nursing home was in receivership with the prospect of new ownership, and some of the staff just didn't give a damn. If we had a problem, it was easier to take care of it ourselves. We became very upset over this, and one night Ray said, "What did we ever do to deserve this? We're supposed to be enjoying our lives at this age and we're stuck in this place where no one gives a damn."

"We had everything," I said, "and had to give it up, and now there's nothing to look forward to."

We cried together, as we had done a few times in the past. There are times when we felt very sorry for ourselves, and I think we'd earned that right. No one really knew our pain. Our dear friends Judy and Joe heard our complaints and sympathized with us, helping in any way they could to make our lives easier. Judy called me nearly every day. I cried on her shoulder so much, and she always told me exactly what she thought. Sometimes it wasn't what I wanted to hear, but I always listened to what she had to say. I have learned that a true friend will be there for you and help you through the roughest times of your life without question. My siblings have also been a strong source of support. I don't know what I would do without them, either. Of course, the girls—Gina, Sam, and Trisha—are always concerned, but they all live far away and are busy with their own lives. I don't want them to worry about us.

Our love for each other has not diminished at all. In fact, I think all this has brought us even closer than we were before, and every single day before I leave, he thanks me for being there with him.

Early in 2010, our community newspaper asked readers to submit love stories to be published on Valentine's Day. My published article is as follows:

> My husband is my hero! He had a tragic accident in our home on Sept. 11, 2004, where he fell and broke his neck and is now a quadriplegic residing in a nursing home. It isn't always a pleasant place to live but with his health issues that require 24-hour care, it's not possible for him to live at home. I stay with him every night because of his needs, and will continue to do whatever I can to make his complicated life a little easier, and to be assured that he gets the care he deserves. He never complains or even gets depressed, and many times he is the one that has to lift my spirits. We have no regrets because we have happy memories of the things we did and are so grateful we didn't put them off until retirement. Even though he's paralyzed, he's still the wonderful guy I met 22 ½ years ago and I love him with all my heart.

Ray and I have had many conversations about the people we encounter every day at this facility. Some we wish would go away and others we'd like to spend more time with. It can actually be a pleasant place when there are people working that we care about and who genuinely care about us. They come in and tell us about their lives and ask our opinions on certain matters. One young nurse even complimented us by saying she hopes she has a marriage as great as ours someday!

In 2011, with the approach of the seventh anniversary of Ray's accident, we were informed that an article would appear in the newspaper. The article was written by the reporter who had written several other articles about us. This one was published on September 4, 2011, and is as follows:

The Long, Impossible Road Home for Ray

As remarkable as quadriplegic Ray Hocking is, his wife, Sandra, is even more remarkable.

Seven years after Ray's inexplicable fall—he was closing the refrigerator door in his Norwich condominium and somehow snapped his neck, causing immediate paralysis—his wife of 24 years is still his best advocate.

"Ray's doing well at this time," Sandra recently wrote in an e-mail. "He was hospitalized twice in July and twice this year with sepsis, along with the constant urinary infections. He's still at the same place, which is under new management … again. It's nothing like when he first went there. Now everyone's in a wheelchair and there are a lot of Alzheimer's patients. It's not a very pleasant place to spend your retirement years. I still stay there every single night and hate it most of the time, but I will not leave him because that's what gets him through each day and night. I told him in the beginning that I would always be here with him and I will never disappoint him. He's too good a person and deserves a lot more than life has to offer him."

She meant it in 1987 when Sandra Occhionero Kent said "for better or worse" when she married Ray Hocking. Since his injury on Sept. 11, 2004, she has devotedly stuck by her husband's side. Next Sunday, when the world marks the 10th anniversary of the 9/11 terrorist attacks, Sandra and Ray Hocking will also mark the seventh anniversary of Ray's becoming a quadriplegic.

He has lived in a nursing home for nearly all of that time, and despite Sandra's early optimism that Ray would return home, that dream has not been realized and likely never will.

A power company lineman for 38 years up until the accident, Ray, 68, is on Medicaid now. He's classified as needing custodial care, meaning someone has to assist with all the daily essentials, including feeding, bathing, toileting, and dressing him.

Sandra said from the start she would get Ray home, and even made their condominium handicapped-accessible, but the severity of Ray's disability has made that impossible. Two years ago when the state hyped its new initiative, "Money Follows the Person," aimed at allowing people to leave nursing homes and return to community living, the Hockings thought it would be their opportunity to get Ray back to the condominium.

"We were disappointed once again as we quickly found out there wasn't enough money to follow this person home!" Sandra wrote.

Ray's care is simply too expensive, and Sandra, who already pays $900 out-of-pocket each month for massages her husband needs, said she can't afford to supplement the state's allowance. She's continued to work as a credit executive at Mohegan Sun, explaining she can't afford to retire, and spends the rest of her time with Ray at the nursing home. It's certainly not the life anyone would choose, but for Sandra, there's not even a question of where she'll go when she gets out of work each day. She spends every night, all night, with her husband.

Ray, she says, has accepted his fate.

But not Sandra.

"There are times when I get depressed about the whole situation and can't understand why this horrible accident happened to this wonderful man," she says. She's kept a journal and some day would like to write a book.

"We have met many wonderful people along this journey and found out who our real friends are who have stood by us through the darkest hours," she says.

Without those people—friends and family—Sandra says she's not sure the couple could have gotten this far.

I met the Hockings not long after Ray's injury and have followed their lives since. What most troubles me is that there is no adequate facility for a person like Ray. He does require special equipment and around-the-clock care, but it's unfortunate that it must be at a convalescent home.

It just seems that there's got to be a better, more cost-effective way to care for a quadriplegic. Some quads are able to go home. I wish Ray was one of them.

Shortly after this article appeared, I received a check for $1,000 from a generous lady that I have never met. A gesture of this magnitude renews my faith in others, knowing there are people in this world that genuinely care about others.

My siblings, Dick, Mike, and Debby, know most of what Ray and I are experiencing because my parents' care is mostly in their hands, since I'm busy caring for Ray. Both of my parents are suffering with health issues and are in an assisted living facility. The situation, however, has brought my siblings and me much closer. We're on the phone with each other several times daily and see one another much more than we ever have before. We love hanging out together, and each of us knows that we can count on the others if the need arises. I have learned, from my own situation that changed my life, what a gift it is to have people that genuinely care. They're also there for Ray whenever he needs them too. During this time, Ray and I have had many conversations about my parents' situation and how it has affected every one of us for such a long time. My siblings and I have joked about my parents being bionic, because it seems that no matter how much their health fails, they bounce right back again. They're amazing for ninety and ninety-one years old.

Sometimes it's difficult to find privacy in Ray's world, and I bought a Do Not Disturb sign to hang on his door when he's having his massages. Even with the door closed, someone will walk in to take his temperature, drop off mail, or perhaps just to see what's going on behind that closed door! Many of our private conversations take place late at night while we're in bed because, at that time, it's less likely someone will open the door and walk in. We talk about everything, even our previous marriages, which we've both confessed have left us with fond memories. I express my concern about Gina being so far away and the hope of seeing her in the near future. We have conversations about our "adopted kids" in New York and wish we could see them more. I express my concern about my siblings and the stress we're all under with my parents' health problems. He talks about his favorite aides or the latest gossip at the nursing home.

We know that some of the experiences we've had since our lives changed have been positive. We've met some wonderful people who will remain friends forever, and Ray has been an inspiration to so many. In our "past life," he was a very private person. He has had to learn to open up with his feelings and say exactly what's on his mind. I've learned that he's quite a comic, always ready to tell a tale or play a joke on someone.

He loves to have fun! One night he even got me to put fart spray on one of the office doorknobs and was a little perturbed when it went unnoticed. He persuaded me to order a "mind molester," which is a tiny battery-operated device that can be placed anywhere. It makes a beeping noise at different intervals, and its purpose is to drive people out of their minds. Right now it's taped to the bottom of his wheelchair. When we told Kim, one of our favorite nurses, about it, she realized it was the noise that had been making her a little crazy for the past few nights. His wheelchair wasn't moving, and though she'd been around it for over seven years, she had never heard that noise before. Unfortunately, she wasn't the one he wanted to drive nuts, but at least he knows it works. And when he has the full attention of the aides, he is loving it! Since he needs two aides to get him in and out of bed, at times a third aide will be in his room, just hanging out. I've told them that Ray's lucky because it's every man's fantasy to have multiple women in his bedroom!

One morning in May 2012, instead of saying his usual, "Sandra, get up. It's seven o'clock," Ray asked, "Are you awake?" When I answered that I was, he said, "I just had a crazy dream." Having been a lineman for so many years, he often dreams about working on power lines. In this dream, as he told it: "I was working high on a pole in Korea and along came Perry Como and Tony Bennett. They each climbed up the pole and we all started singing to the Korean people while standing on top of the pole. After a while the pole fell down and we had to replace it. With Perry and Tony's help, we put up another pole that same day!"

Well, that got me out of bed quick because I was laughing so hard.

We know how lucky we are to have found each other after fearing we would never have another chance at love. We had many wonderful times in those seventeen years before the accident and created some great memories, for which we feel fortunate. As we've recently celebrated our silver anniversary, we reminisce with videos and letters we wrote to each other and know that there was—and still is—a lot to be thankful for. But there are also so many things we miss that others take for granted. We miss sitting next to each other on the couch, as we did on so many evenings. I miss lying next to him in bed, when his body would warm me on those cold winter nights. I miss him being in our home and cooking our favorite meals together, and the margaritas and martinis he used to make for me. I miss the love notes he would often leave me, and the romantic dinners he cooked and served with candles on the table. The last love note he left was on the basement door. When I pulled into the garage after work on the night of the accident, I saw a note on the door that lead from the garage to the basement. It simply said "I love you, Raymond." That note has never been touched and will remain on that door until I leave my home for good.

One of my last memories of him in our home was that Saturday morning, when he came to say good-bye before he left for work. I was still in bed, as it was early, before seven. Since our water bed was very low, he got down on his knees and kissed me, which he did every morning before leaving the house. Sadly, that was the last time he was in our bedroom. He will never see it again because it is located on the second floor.

Even after all these years, I get angry all over again when I think of the things that were taken away from us as we were planning to retire and travel. I'm envious of other people whose dreams of the future are fulfilled when their years of work are done and they have the free time to do whatever they desire. Ray misses what we could have had too, but has accepted it better than me.

Sometimes when we hear an upsetting remark directed at one or both of us, we wish that person could be in our place for one day—twenty-four hours—and then perhaps his or her anger could be directed elsewhere.

I don't know why we were the chosen ones to be dealt this hand. It is said that there's a reason for everything, and I've tried to figure out what could be the reason for this. Perhaps it's to show me that I am as strong as people tell me I am   or for Ray and Gina to have a caring relationship   or for Ray to inspire others … or for me to become aware of my writing skills. One thing both of us miss is the newfound intimacy we were experiencing as we grew older.

We've accepted that he will never be able to go home to live, so this has become the room where we have all our private moments.

CHAPTER 8

All about Me

We must be willing to let go of the life we've planned, so as to have the life that is waiting for us. Joseph Campbell

While sitting in the emergency room, I remember thinking that this cannot be happening. You read about this, you see it on TV, but you never think it's going to happen to you. We had saved and planned carefully for retirement. We were talking about moving out west and trying to decide on our final destination when our future was shattered. No one can ever be prepared for a life-changing event of this magnitude. I don't know the exact moment I realized how drastically my future had changed. I think I was just going through the motions, doing what I thought was expected of me. How does one adjust?

I tried to become available to everyone, especially Ray, because I knew he needed me more than he ever had before. It was also important that the medical staff be able to consult with me whenever they needed to. I made a point to have someone with me whenever I spoke to a doctor, because I didn't want to take the chance of misinterpreting pertinent information. As soon as Ray was out of

CCU, my father suggested I consult his lawyer. He accompanied me on my initial visit. I immediately liked his attorney and knew I could trust her to guide me in all legal matters. After I explained my situation, she said she would begin preparing the legal documents that would give me the power to make all of our decisions. This was getting very frightening, and I wondered, Will I be able to do this?

When it was time to make the power of attorney official, I asked my father and a hospital respiratory therapist to witness, along with the notary public. It was one of the hardest things I'd ever done. I was asked to help my now paralyzed husband "make an X" by placing a pen in one of his nonfunctioning hands. This was the beginning of the end of his independence, and it brought tears to my eyes to see my life partner suddenly so dependent on me. This was so unfair! If things happen for a reason, what could the reason be for this?

The night before his transfer to the rehabilitation facility, knowing I was going to a place far away from home for what was going to be a long time, I was very emotional. My immediate future was unknown, and that was scary. I spent the night with Ray at the hospital as I had done since he was moved out of CCU. I woke up early and went to the waiting room so I wouldn't disturb him. When I returned to the room, I noticed his respiratory rate. He had woken up and gotten very nervous when he realized I wasn't there.

By the time we said our good-byes, thanked the hospital staff, and made the hour trip to the rehabilitation facility, it was 1:45 p.m. My sister and brother brought my car so I could ride in the ambulance with Ray. After he was evaluated by the staff, I left the room and starting crying. It had been such an emotional day, and now my siblings would have to leave and I would be all by myself. I just wanted to go home!

I quickly discovered that showering every day was out of the question. For me, a shower once or twice a day was part of my everyday life. However, the individual rooms were not equipped with showers, so every morning for about the first two weeks, I gathered my clean clothes and all my body lotions, went into the public bathrooms, and took what Ray called a field shower. Anyone in the military knows what that is! During that time, on the days when I got to go home for a few hours, I would jump in the shower and welcome that flow of soothing hot water. I let it run until I thought the pipes would go dry. After that, I was introduced to the showers in the pool area and was able to shower daily again. Ray and I often talk about that because when we drove across the country, as we did several times, I absolutely demanded that we stay in motels with clean rooms, showers, and a king-size bed with clean sheets. During the times that Ray has been in the hospitals, I've slept on chairs, cots, and couches. How priorities change! One night at the nursing home, when he was sick, I sat in a chair all night long. When he went to the hospital in the morning, I sat in another chair in the emergency room for about twelve hours, until he was finally brought to a room. I stayed there with him all night long. That time I was in the same clothes for almost forty-eight hours!

The first time I actually felt sorry for myself was on our third day at the rehabilitation facility. It was hard to sleep on their uncomfortable cots, especially when the staff had to come in the room and turn him every two hours.

The first few nights I couldn't sleep, and my mind wandered back to happier days right before the accident. My niece Dina had had a baby in May, and I had offered to take care of her on my days off so Dina could go back to work part-time. I immediately fell in love with baby Madison and looked forward to being with her. I bonded with Madison by singing "Rock a-bye Baby" whenever she cried, and she always stopped and listened to me. One day in the hospital when Ray was in intensive care and Dina and Madison were with Gina and me in the waiting room, Madison wouldn't stop crying. I took her, put her head on my shoulder, and started singing softly in her little ear. It was the first time my daughter had seen me with the baby, and she thought it was amazing how Madison recognized my voice. Unfortunately, my bonding with Madison ended when she was only four months old because of Ray's accident. Shortly after that, Madison and her parents moved to Florida. After six weeks they realized it wasn't what they'd expected and decided to come back to Connecticut. Since I had a large condo and was hardly ever there, they moved in until they found a place of their own. I looked forward to seeing Madison every morning before going to work. After they moved out, I saw less and less of her. Her parents didn't feel that the nursing home was a good environment for her and my free time was limited, so it was difficult for me to visit her.

After a couple of weeks at the rehabilitation hospital, I was still tired most of the time. Actually, I had never been so tired in all my life. Sometimes when I would just start to fall asleep, Ray would need me to scratch an itch or get him a drink. I wanted to scream at those times but couldn't, because it wasn't his fault that he couldn't do things for himself. My parents kept telling me to go home and get some sleep in my own bed. They didn't seem to realize, or couldn't understand, that I just couldn't leave him alone. He needed me! No one could give him the constant care that I could, and I wanted to make sure I was available for whatever he needed. Not only was he unable to use his hands, he couldn't speak because of the respirator and could only make a sound with his lips to get my attention.

Every time I went home, I had several e-mails waiting for me from friends and relatives who wanted to be kept abreast of our situation. I enjoyed the quiet alone time I spent on the computer, but it seemed to pass so quickly. Before I knew it, it would be time to leave again.

I was so exhausted and stressed that one day on my way home, I got lost and could not find my way home. This was a route I had already driven several times without incident. My sister happened to call right then, and I told her I didn't think I was ever going to see my home again. She called my brother, who was working in New Hampshire, and he immediately called me and told me to go to the nearest gas station and ask what town I was in. I knew that was going to make me look like an idiot, not having any idea where I was, but I had to do it. Then my brother guided me home. Three hours later, I arrived at my home from a ride that normally took me fifty-five minutes. That was my first meltdown.

I turned sixty while Ray was at the hospital recovering from his flap surgery. His cousin Lois was visiting from Pennsylvania. We had agreed that on our way home that evening, we would meet my sister for a drink at a bar in our hometown. What no one knew was that Ray had told me that I was actually going to a surprise birthday celebration with family and friends. I must have looked really surprised, because to this day no one knows that I faked it.

I returned to work on Saturday, December 18, 2004, after a leave of absence of twelve weeks, and Ray returned to the rehabilitation facility on December 23, 2004. It was good to get back to work and to a more structured daily life. I stayed at home during my work week, and then left on Tuesday morning to spend my days off with him. I returned home on Wednesday night, since my work week began on Thursday.

When it came time to pay our 2004 income taxes, I could not believe the amount I had to pay. . The following years haven't been much different. I've had to make phone calls to retrieve my state refund, explaining the situation because I always get notifications that I owe an outstanding debt. I thought I had finally gotten to the bottom of that when I spoke to a gentleman in October 2011, who told me it was for the "employee that comes into your home to help with your husband's care which you have never acknowledged." I wanted to say, "Where the f- - k did you get that idea?" but being the classy lady I'm told I am, I assured him that Ray has been residing in a nursing home since the day he left the rehabilitation hospital. The man said they were under the impression that Ray was living at home with assistance. He assured me it would be taken care of and I should not have a problem in the future. However, when I filed my state taxes in 2012 for a refund of less than $400, I received a Notice of Refund Offset from the Department of Revenue Services. It stated: "We have determined you have one or more liabilities that are currently outstanding and all or a portion of your individual income tax refund for the period ending 12/31/2011 was credited to the liability or liabilities listed:" Not again … I'm so sick of this crap! It was almost not worth it to go through all this again, but I was determined that they were not going to get another dime of my money.

My wonderful accountant works very hard each year figuring out my complicated income tax and never charges me a penny. He says I have enough to worry about, calling it a gesture of good will. Finally, after six years, not even knowing what he charges, I offered him a check because, in this troubled economy, every dollar counts. I certainly appreciate that he was sympathetic to my situation, and I will never forget that. I have and will continue to refer clients to him.

After the spend down was completed, I was informed that I could accumulate assets, in my name only, without being investigated for having "too much money."

My second meltdown happened when Ray had been at the nursing home for only a few months. Again, I was stressed and walked in to see Ray sitting, almost reclining, in a Geri Chair, looking very much like an old man. I proceeded to tell anyone in earshot that I didn't want him in that chair. I wanted him in a wheelchair so he could sit up and look around. Someone told me to calm down. I yelled right back that they were not to tell me to calm down. I was looking out for Ray's best interest and that was not to have him always sitting in that stupid chair!

Of course, my outburst upset Ray, and he said if he could get out of the *stupid* chair, he would jump right out the window! Well, the wrong ears heard that remark, and a few days later he was talking to a psychologist, unbeknownst to him. He thought a man was just making friendly conversation by pulling up a chair and sitting alongside him—until we got the bill! The facility had requested psychological visits for Ray without our knowledge, which were held in the visiting area at the nursing home and were called "office visits."

I went to Minneapolis with Sam for Gina's thirtieth birthday The weather was very cooperative, with temperatures in the high seventies. Sandals and tank top weather—for the young ones, of course, not me. We partied hardy all weekend long. The first night, after Gina had opened her gifts, we went to a Thai restaurant for dinner. We headed straight to the bar for before dinner drinks, which were pina coladas served in coconuts.

The next day we shopped till we dropped at the Mall of America, where Sam and I had our caricatures sketched, and then it was uptown for more shopping. That evening we went to a club in St. Paul for Gina's birthday celebration. Her friends from Connecticut were in a band and they came especially to play at this event. On our last night we went to a vintage hippy-type place where a guitar player was playing Bob Dylan songs. It was a very relaxing, enjoyable evening.

I knew I would have a teary good-bye if I saw Gina the next day before I left, so I told her to sleep in and I would call her when I got home. I loved being in Minneapolis with her and always had such a good time with her friends, even though leaving her made me so sad because I knew it would be quite some time before I would be able to visit again. Wild horses couldn't have kept me away this time, because turning thirty is such an important birthday and I wanted to share it with her. I knew it pleased her that I was there. I'd felt like I'd somewhat neglected her since the beginning of this ordeal.

On April 20, 2005, Ray's former wife called me after finding out about his accident from her brother, whom I had contacted at Ray's request. He thought the family would like to know of his situation, since he'd always had a good relationship with them. She was very pleasant, and we had a good conversation as I told her about the accident. She told me she was still mourning the passing of her second husband, which was very difficult for her. She promised to call and speak with Ray later that evening, but she did not call. I feel so bad when people he cares about disappoint him.

A month later, I went to the town hall to meet with the city planner about the handicapped ramp my brother wanted to build at our condo. I signed several papers and was told to mail certified letters to the abutting property owners for the zoning meeting on June 17. I started to cry because it meant I had to go to the post office and take more time out of my already busy day to do something I didn't have time for. After mailing the letters, I left the post office and saw a police officer placing a ticket on my car's windshield. When I asked what it was for, she said I was parked too close to a pedestrian crosswalk. I told her my car had not been there more than six minutes, but she didn't care. I guess I had been too tired to see the sign. When I got home there was a call on my answering machine telling me it wasn't necessary to send out the letters after all. After taking a closer look at the drawing of the proposed ramp, the city planner decided a variance was not needed. The application was withdrawn and notices would be sent out once again, telling my neighbors to disregard the prior notice.

I was really upset about receiving the parking ticket, so I immediately wrote a letter to the Public Parking Commission. I explained my situation and asked if they could make an exception for me this one time. Surprisingly, I got a reply expressing their sorrow and telling me that they would not enforce the ticket, and that I was to take care of myself, which was more important than paying a fine at this time. I called and thanked them, expressing my gratitude while realizing, once again, there *are* kind and thoughtful people in this world who are willing to help others.

After my brother began erecting the handicapped ramp, which would be fifty feet long and run alongside our condo and up to the deck in the back, a neighbor who lived in a unit in back of mine complained to the town that I didn't have a building permit. It seems that she didn't like the way the ramp looked, which didn't make much sense to me. All she could see when she looked out her front door was the back of my building. There was absolutely no view at all! I got a call from the building department and had to pay $30 for a building permit, which I made sure I posted so the nosey neighbor could see it. When I neglected to put my trash barrel back in the garage after a trash pickup because I was hardly ever home, she moved it out of sight because she didn't like looking at it. There was even a sign on it that said, Put me away, I stink. She apparently was missing something in her life, because she spent so much time worrying about mine. She had no idea what I went through each day, and that the garbage pail being put away was not on my list of priorities. Perhaps I should have spent more time trying to make my neighbors happy instead of trying to take care of my husband and myself.

My time was limited, and on my days off I tried to spend as much of it with Ray as I could.. I felt so bad that he had to be there twenty-four hours a day. Plus, I enjoyed being with him, which was something many people couldn't understand. I was told that I should be sleeping at home, but what they didn't realize was that I did not enjoy sleeping at home, alone in my bed, because being there did not seem like a home anymore. It was just an empty shell, and I avoided going there as much as possible. We had been in our new condo for only nine months before the accident and had not created many memories, so it truly didn't feel like home without him there. Another thing I was told was to "take time for myself." I never failed to have my nails and hair done, which were things I looked forward to. Someone at the nursing home thought I could use a massage, so I scheduled one and thoroughly enjoyed it. It relaxed me so much and made me feel so good, I decided to continue them on a regular basis.

In November 2005, my special friend Samanthia, whom I depended on for many things, mainly moral support, moved to Saratoga, New York. Now I really felt alone. I knew I was going to miss her tremendously, but tried not to let her know just how much. I didn't want to put a damper on her happiness, since she felt bad enough about leaving me. We had met about seven years earlier, when we began working together. I had liked her immediately but had not known how very special she would become to me. In our conversations I learned that her mom was deceased, her dad was remarried, and she lived with her sister Trisha and Trisha's two-year-old daughter Nya. When Samanthia told me of her mom's illness and unfortunate death, I admired those two young women, who were in their early twenties, trying to make a life for themselves and Nya without a mother's guidance. Throughout these years, they have succeeded. They've had a few disappointments, like their dad's death in 2007, which meant that they were completely on their own.

When Ray was injured, our lives really came together. It didn't take much time for me to realize how much I liked these girls, and little Nya, and how very much I wanted—and needed—them in my life. They felt the same about me, and as they spent time with Ray, we grew to love one another as family. They have given me so much support. Both became nurses and they understand Ray's condition, which has helped me cope at the most difficult times. I knew I was going to miss them tremendously when they moved, but I also knew it wasn't a decision they had made in haste. One Mother's Day I received this note from Trisha:

> I couldn't find a card that could describe what you mean to our family so I just thought we would write it down and tell you. We all want to thank you for taking us in as your "adopted" family. All three of us are lucky to have you and Ray as part of our lives. You have done more for us than you can ever imagine and on this Mother's Day we just wanted you to know that we appreciate you. You're always listening and giving us advice and housing and feeding us when we come down and we are grateful for that. You are more family to us then we could have ever hoped for. I hope you enjoy your day and please know that we are always thinking about you and Ray. We love you. Trisha, Nya and Sam

On another Mother's Day, I received this note from Sam:

> I looked and looked for a card for you at CVS, Brooks, and Wal-Mart but could not find a card that expressed how I feel so I decided not to buy you a card. I just wanted to let you know on this Mother's Day that you are so many things to me no card could ever put into words. You have opened your heart, your family, and your friendship to me which I will be forever grateful. Gina is very, very lucky to have a mother like you, and I realize I am very lucky to have a friend like you. I know that you will stick by me no matter what and that is more than anyone can ever ask for. I have found something in you that I have found in no one else and nothing can ever be said enough about what kind of person you are. I hope you know that I will always be there for you just like you are for me.
>
> Happy Mother's Day!!! Love, Samanthia

These girls are so thoughtful. It warms my heart to know how much they think of me. I am so glad they came into my life at a time when I needed them, and that we all grew to love each other as family. Ray has wholeheartedly welcomed them into our lives as well, and we can't imagine our life without them.

Sam's boyfriend of several years also decided to make the move to New York. They visit as often as they can. When Trisha decided to go to nursing school, she applied for, and received, a grant from the state. The next year, Sam followed in her footsteps. Shortly after Sam started nursing school, she called to tell me she was going to make me a "grandmother." This was good news, because it gave us all something new and wonderful to focus on. I had given up all hope of ever becoming a grandmother, since my daughter made it perfectly clear that she has no interest in becoming a mother. Sam's son Carter was born on September 4, 2009, and he calls Ray and me Nana and Papa. Nya became a teenager in March and has blossomed into a beautiful and sweet young lady, and I love her and call her my granddaughter. On May 10, 2010, I wrote a letter for Nya to bring to her teacher, because I couldn't make it to New York to go to "grandmother's day" at her school. I wanted her to know that, since she felt comfortable enough to invite me, I would acknowledge the day, even though I couldn't attend.

> I wish I could be there to spend "grandmother's day" with Nya because it would make her very happy, but since I can't be there in person, I would like to say that I have been blessed to "adopt" her as my granddaughter. She makes me very happy, and I think she is one of the sweetest young girls I have had the pleasure to know and am honored to be her "Nana." I have known her since she was a very little girl, and I am proud of the bright and charming young lady she is now and am looking forward to a long and happy future together.
>
> Sandra Hocking …otherwise known as "Nana"

Ray was in the hospital on our eighteenth wedding anniversary with a urinary tract infection. I spent part of the day at the hospital before going to have my nails done. I was so tired, I almost fell asleep at the wheel. I actually did nod off while my nails were being polished. When I got home, my parents brought a bouquet of beautiful flowers. After they left, I went to bed by myself. *Happy Anniversary!*

On our nineteenth anniversary, on August 2, 2006, Ray was in the hospital again, this time for pneumonia. When I arrived that morning, he had a beautiful bouquet of yellow roses and a lovely card waiting for me. A friend, who had visited the day before, had told Ray she would make sure the flowers would be there before I arrived. It made him so happy that he was able to give me an anniversary surprise. Thank goodness for thoughtful friends.

It has been over eight years since the accident, and I still feel angry much of the time. I'm frustrated, tired, and emotionally exhausted. When Ray was hospitalized for the second time in a week in July 2006, he seemed more agitated than normal and told me he missed having someone to talk to. I cried all the way home. Once I had to stop because the tears were blocking my view. At the hospital one morning before work, I broke a fingernail and started to bawl. It just seemed that nothing good ever happened, that there were no positives in our lives, nothing to look forward to except going back to the nursing home.

I knew I had to get out of the funk I was in, but didn't know what to do. Deep down I knew that the base of all my stress was not the situation itself, but that I felt the people closest to me had distanced themselves from me and it was eating me up. Ray's famous words kept echoing in my mind: don't try to change something you can't. My best friend Judy also told me basically the same thing. She always has good things to say about everyone, and keeps telling me that people just don't know what to say or do in an extreme situation such as ours. I couldn't believe that, because at that time the "situation" was two years old.

In April of 2007, one of my friends at work retired. I applied for her shift, which was basically the same as mine, but with Friday and Saturday off. I thought it would be good to be away from the casino on the weekends, and I needed a change from my Monday-Tuesday "weekend." The only problem was that on Sundays the hours were 8:00 a.m. to 4:00 p.m. I thought perhaps I could sleep home on Saturday nights, and my brother Dick could go to the nursing home to feed Ray on Sunday mornings and spend a little time with him, since I couldn't be there. Dick agreed, and my sister Debby said she would go on the Sunday of the weekends that she had off. I thought perhaps I could eventually switch my Sunday hours with Gary, a coworker and friend. He had agreed to do that, since he worked 12:30 p.m. to 8:30 p.m. However, our director had other ideas. He said he couldn't change hours just to suit me. WTF! Other departments did it, but he was not going to budge. I told him that all my other coworkers had been very supportive during this difficult situation, and they would not object to something that would make my life a little easier. He still wouldn't budge. I'm glad he couldn't read my mind that day! He finally said that we could switch once a month. It was very, very difficult, because when Saturday night rolled around, Ray started to get nervous. I ended up staying at the nursing home and then would get up at 5:00 a.m. and go home to get ready for work. By the time I got back to the nursing home in the late afternoon, I just wanted to pass out from exhaustion. In 2010 my director resigned and the acting director, who was also my immediate boss, instantly changed those Sunday hours. Thank you, Debi!

Not only have some of my coworkers been helpful to me, they've also been accommodating to Ray. Gary worked with me for several years and visits Ray and supplies him with his favorite candy, black licorice. He has also helped Ray to understand his iPad. Rein has also worked with me for many years and visits Ray. Since both are interested in history and politics, Ray enjoys his conversations with Rein. Each of these men have become my good friends, and I know I can count on them if I ever have the need in the future. That's a very good feeling! Other coworkers, past and present, have also been kind enough to visit Ray. Debi even supplies him with homemade soupy on occasion! Several have come to his birthday celebrations too. I have to say, they have all been understanding and have provided a tremendous amount of emotional support for me. I feel privileged that I have worked with the greatest group of people during the most challenging time of my life.

In February 2008, when Samanthia, Trisha, and Nya were staying at my place on one of their weekend visits, the shower was leaking through the kitchen ceiling. Plus, there was water in the garage every time it rained, the garbage disposal wasn't working, and three burners on the stove wouldn't light. I couldn't imagine how everything was going to get fixed because my brother was working out of town. However, he was able to come over, check out the shower stall, and said he would come back with tools. I told him and Sam that probably the best thing for me to do was sell the condo so I wouldn't have to worry about every little thing. Of course, after I mentioned this to Ray, he didn't think it was a very good idea, even when I told him how overwhelmed I felt with my everyday life and all the things going wrong at home. I mentioning all of this to my friend at work, Ericka, and she said she and her husband would be glad to help me out. So with a little help from my friends, the shower stall got fixed, a new garbage disposal was put in, the burners on the stove were repaired, and dealt with the water problem in my garage. Ericka also comes over whenever necessary and cleans my house to make sure it's always ready for overnight guests. Ericka and her husband became my special angels.

During the early morning hours of Sunday, May 28, Ray's catheter was leaking and neither the LPN or the RN could get another inserted after a few tries. So it was a trip to the ER, then a call to the urologist who took his sweet time getting to the hospital. His attempt was successful, and then Ray had to have two doses of antibiotics by IV to ward off any infection. After about six hours, it was back to the nursing home for Ray, and I went home to change. A few days later, again in the early morning hours, the new catheter started leaking again. Without hesitation, Ray suggested they send him to the hospital. I was livid, because the last place I wanted to spend my day off was in the emergency room. I well knew what it entailed for me whenever he was taken there: hours and hours of sitting, waiting, pacing, reading, napping. I called my brother from the car while waiting for the ambulance to get there. He wanted to come get me and take me to the hospital, but I would not let him. He knew I was in a bad way and didn't think I could drive. I told him I would be fine and refused to let him come as I needed to have my own car available. I just wanted to yell, **No, I don't want to go to that damn hospital again!**

I arrived at the emergency room about forty-five minutes after Ray. I was already copping an attitude by that time, and when I arrived at his cubicle, I noticed his hand was on the call bell. I was livid. He'd been in this place many, many times as a quadriplegic, so what were they thinking? I was ready to castrate someone and knew that I could in the state of mind I was in!

One night at the nursing home, Ray woke up shortly after midnight, realizing his blood pressure was very low. He woke me, and I moved his legs up and down rapidly to get the blood flowing. I took his pressure, and it registered at 54/30. He called the nurse and told her he needed to get to the hospital. He knew he needed an IV of saline solution, which helps to increase the blood pressure by adding fluid to his system. He told the nurse that if they had someone who was IV certified, he wouldn't need to go to the hospital. The nurse simply made out the paperwork and called the ambulance to transport him.

Of course I was thinking of myself and how tired I was, knowing that I wasn't going to get any more sleep that night. I kept my mouth shut because I knew if I said anything, I would regret it later. So, we went to the hospital, he in the ambulance and me in my car. As usual, it was so cold in that emergency room. Thank goodness we had again brought our own blankets After the first couple of hours, they decided to test Ray's blood and urine, and told us the results would be ready in about an hour and a half. By this time it was 2:30 a.m. and I still hadn't had any sleep. Of course, the final result was a urinary tract infection, which we knew and had told them he always had one, but nevertheless, they admitted him about six, so I went home. I had such a chill from being there, I had to put a heavy blanket around me to keep warm. I slept for about two hours, showered and changed, and went back to the hospital.

That same week I noticed that his right big toe looked infected. I was planning to make an appointment with his podiatrist when I received a call from the nursing home. The podiatrist was in that morning but wouldn't be able to do anything for Ray because of an unpaid bill of $72! My reply was, "You should be ashamed of yourself for letting one of your own suffer because of $72." That charge ended up being in dispute. After going over my previous bills, I realized I had been charged twice for the same service, and I refused to pay. I guess my little speech helped, because Ray called a short time later and told me his toe had been taken care of.

When sleep is impossible at the nursing home, you can't get up and walk around like you can in your own home. Instead you lie there and think, and cry, and wish things were different. One night I grabbed my Blackberry phone and sent an e-mail to Gina and Sam:

> Here I am again, lying awake since before 5:00 a.m. with a ton of things going on inside my head and wondering what lies ahead in this new day. My shoulders are so tense—I haven't had a massage since last winter—never seem to find the time. I guess I'm always complaining which I never did in my old life and I'm sorry for that. I just think of what a great life I'd be having if this fucking accident hadn't happened and most of the time I'm mad at the world because of it. Well, it's almost 7a.m. so I'll be able to get up now and begin that brand new day!

At one point I was so stressed, I wasn't eating much and had panic attacks when I could sleep. At least I thought they were panic attacks. I woke up gasping for breath and was afraid to go back to sleep, which scared the living shit out of me. Shortly after one of these episodes, I stayed overnight in the hotel at work during a snowstorm. I roomed with a friend, who noticed that I sometimes stopped breathing during sleep. It turned out I have sleep apnea, which was discovered when I took a sleep study. I had an appointment to return so I could be shown how to use an apparatus that addressed the apnea, but of all things, we had a nor'easter snowstorm that evening in October and I cancelled the appointment.

With the stress in my life compounded with my parents' health problems, I feel that sometimes I just don't have a chance to relax and get a much needed night's sleep. I finally had a chance to return for the second part of the sleep program. A small mask was placed over my nose and a machine was turned on. After an hour I made the tech take it off because I could hardly breathe. She said the bigger one that fit over my nose and mouth was probably what I needed. I tolerated it for about four hours, but then had to get out from under it because I felt like I was smothering. When I went for my consultation with the doctor a few weeks later, I was prepared to tell him I couldn't follow this through. Surprisingly, he told me I had a mild to moderate case of apnea and I wouldn't need to wear the apparatus. He wants to see me in six months to see if I have any lingering issues. Thankfully, I won't have to contend with this at the nursing home every night!

One Saturday afternoon in July, when Ray was in the hospital and I was in his room talking on my phone, my heart suddenly started beating rapidly. I could actually see my blouse moving. I told Ray to call for the nurse. She immediately took my blood pressure, which was highly elevated, along with the fast pounding of my heart. I didn't think I was having a heart attack because I felt fine. I knew this had to be a serious matter, though, because I was put on a stretcher and taken to the emergency room.

We're familiar with the emergency room staff, and I knew and liked the doctor assigned to me. He gave me an injection to bring my heart rate down. I was also given medication to keep my blood pressure from elevating in the future. Someone had called my sister and brother, and they arrived looking very concerned. When they saw me looking normal, they were greatly relieved. Meanwhile, I knew Ray was upstairs extremely worried, so I had someone call and let him know that I was all right and would be coming back upstairs when I was released from the emergency room.

The following Monday I went to see a cardiologist. He scheduled a stress test, an echocardiogram, and a twenty-minute session, where a huge machine took pictures of my heart. All tests were normal, but when I consulted with the cardiologist, he said I had a condition I had been born with that could be easily corrected with a procedure he'd performed several times. He gave me a prescription so I could continue the medication they'd given me in the hospital and told me to consider having the procedure done. This condition would not kill me, but if it happened again, it could occur at a very inopportune time. I considered myself lucky that it had first happened while I was in the hospital.

Later that evening, after my visit with Ray ended, I went home. I was very nervous being by myself. I thought that at least if I was at the nursing home, where I would be if Ray weren't in the hospital, there would be nurses present in case it happened again. I tried to read, but my mind was wandering and I kept wondering what I would do if it happened while I was alone? The doctor's answer had been to call 911. Do not try to drive myself to the hospital. I could also put my face in a bucket of ice! I guess that would shock my system and my heart rate would go down—so I put a large bowl full of ice cubes beside my bed. This continued until Ray was released, and I went back to sleeping at the nursing home. When I had to see the doctor to renew my medication, he said as long as I hadn't had another episode and was feeling fine with no other symptoms, I could continue with the medication until my next appointment.

Ray has relatives and several friends who are very religious, but they know not to talk religion to me. I feel that if there is a higher power that let this *thing* happen to paralyze this wonderful man forever and ruin the life and plans we had for the future, I can't justify praying. I've been told so many times that we're never given more than we can handle. Well, my life has even more stress now that my parents had to give up my childhood home and move into an assisted living facility. I just want to yell, Stop! I want my old life back!

After visiting my parents with my sister during Christmastime 2011, I was getting in my car when she handed me an envelope.

Before driving away, I opened the envelope. It contained several gift cards with a note that said:

> These are not XMAS gifts, they're to show my appreciation of you keeping the family close. You spend a lot of your own money getting everyone together: it's time someone did something for you without you seeing it coming! As soon as this mess is over and Gina has had time to settle in, we'll go out and see her in California! Thanks for all that you have done this year, you're doing a fabulous job and Mom would be very proud of you! Love you, Deb

She was referring to the sibling gatherings we'd had recently with our brothers Dick and Mike and our significant others, Ray, Jody, Bob, and Janice. We have children that live in other states and can't always be with us, so I want the four of us to stay together. I've seen in so many instances, when the "old folks" are no longer available, the family traditions that were always important no longer seem to matter. The remaining family members don't take the initiative to carry on. I do not want that to happen in our family, because through the years we've spent many wonderful times together and we all want that to continue. We've learned to appreciate one another and love one another for what we're going through. It's the first time we haven't been able to consult our parents and we have had to lean on each other. We've also had a lot of laughs reminiscing about our childhood.

We've all seen paralyzed people out in public in wheelchairs without ever thinking about their daily lives and how they are able to get in and out of those wheelchairs. It's not an easy process, and my heart breaks every time Ray has to go through the motions of getting up and being put to bed. I wish I could give him some of my energy so he could at least use one hand! Again I want to cry, It's just not fair!

I hate it that we have to "live" in a skilled nursing facility. That time I told a resident to "shut up" because he was being rude and obnoxious to the aides, and was yelling so loudly he disturbed Ray's visitors, the supervisor accused me of "resident abuse" and reported me to the administrator, the police, the ombudsman, and the State Board of Health. The administrator told me it was a "very serious" situation, and if it happened again I would no longer be allowed in the facility. Like I would leave Ray here without me. Ain't gonna happen!

I went to the police station to see what the report said, and was told that the officer didn't believe a report was warranted and not to worry about it. Then I had to talk to the social worker at the nursing home to review "residents rights." She was just following protocol and actually sympathized with me. She couldn't believe the aggravation and added stress this put in my already crazy life. Sometimes I hate this place! I've left in tears many mornings because I've had to leave Ray in the care of some people I do not trust. Where is the justice in our lives?

In May 2012, apparently there was a need to save money, so nurses and aides were told there would be a round of layoffs. Ray and I didn't understand how that could be possible because of the last-minute calls the staff had to make to replace the many daily call-outs. I get so aggravated at that place because whenever changes are made, it affects the residents' care.

Several of our friends asked if we had ever considered transferring because whenever they visited loved ones in another facility they found it pleasant and accommodating. I told them you need to spend more than an hour or two a week to know what really goes on in a nursing home. Try spending twelve or twenty-four hours a day for eight years! Besides, Ray is in a private room which allows me to stay with him and if he were to transfer to another facility, that could change.

I'm still tired every day of my life. Bedtime is very late and morning comes too fast. I get annoyed when I hear someone say how tired they are, especially a young person. I want to say to them, you have no idea what it's like to be so tired that you fall asleep in front of your computer at work or at a red light with your foot on the brake. Or perhaps reading in the lunch room and your book falls out of your hands. I've been reduced to tears because I've been so tired in the morning when I get up, and don't know how I will make it through the fourteen hours until I return. When I feel I can't go on, I see the look on Ray's face when he sees me walk through his door in the evening—and that's what makes it all worthwhile.

It's been over eight years since Ray's horrible accident, and I'm still angry. I feel guilty for wanting this whole situation to be over so I can live a fairly normal life again, because I know there's only one way that's going to happen. So I try to go on each and every day and keep up the pace I've been able to endure all this time. However, I can feel that my body is running out of steam now that I'm older. Some days I'm so tired by the end of my work day, I don't know how I'll ever make it until 11:00 p.m. But somehow I get a burst of energy that enables me to keep going. After all, Ray's stuck in the nursing home without getting to smell fresh air for days at a time. And I know, without a doubt, if the situation were reversed and I was the paralyzed one, he would be there for me.

I'm very happy for my "little girl," who recently turned thirty-seven and is enjoying her new home in Los Angeles. I have a heavy heart because I haven't seen her in over a year, which is the longest I've gone without being with her, and I don't know when we'll be together again. I can't get away right now with all my life issues, and she has that wonderful new job. I don't expect her to be coming home anytime in the near future. Sometimes I think I may never see her again.

I don't know when this journey will end, but I know I will be here until Ray draws his last breath, and I'll do whatever it takes to get me through until that time comes. Because as I said, he would do it for me. When I took those marriage vows, I said until death do us part. But not only that, I love him with all my heart And who knows. He may outlive me!

I can't go back to yesterday—because
I was a different person then.
Lewis Carroll

S o many wonderful people have helped us along this journey. If their names have been omitted from my story, it was intentional. I did not want to offend anyone or enter incorrect information. Some people may not want their names or positions publicized, and I can appreciate that. However, Ray and I are grateful to everyone who has come to our aid during this time and will *never* be forgotten.

This *split second* life change has been quite an experience for us, our family, and our close friends. Those who knew us before the accident saw how it transformed us into people we wouldn't recognize from our past life. It has made me a strong, self-reliant, dependable caregiver. I have learned never to take things for granted, because it can all come to an end in that one split second when you least expect it and change your life forever.

Ray's life change has transformed him into a person with a different demeanor. He is much mellower, which seems impossible considering the circumstances. In Gina's own words, "he seemed angry" much of the time in the past. He's gotten used to his situation a lot better than anyone imagined, and because of it, he's become an inspiration to everyone he meets. He looks forward to each new day which he considers a gift. He was more of a loner before, and now he loves being surrounded by people, especially if he can make them laugh!

I have had a gut-full of this health system that I've had to deal with for eight years and wish there was something I could do to change it. A person doesn't really know how it works until there's a loved one involved. I feel sorry for anyone who is in his or her right frame of mind and has to live in a nursing home because of something that happened beyond their control. Many times throughout these years, I have contacted the ombudsman, the corporate office, the regional director, and the State of Connecticut on issues that I knew needed attention, and the only positive response I've received is from the State, which finally contacted me regarding my concerns.

I wish Ray could live the rest of his life at home but, because of our wonderful world of health care, it will never happen. It would be great to be in our own home once again and away from the "skilled nursing facility."

I love you just the way you are. You are my hero!

Ray is the bravest man I know. He's been through more in the last eight years than anyone should have to go through in a complete lifetime ... and he *never complains*! He continues to inspire everyone he meets with his positive attitude, quick wit, good sense of humor, and unbroken spirit, in spite of all he's been through since his accident, especially being confined to a nursing home forever. He is happy to be alive and accepts each new day as a gift. He thanks me every single day for being with him, and he knows that I will remain by his side "for as long as we both shall live." And I know, without a doubt, if the situation were reversed, he would do the same for me. I commend him on the way he's handled this change in our lives, and I love him with all my heart!